A Wise Geek's Guide To Everything

Michael Pollick

Published by Michael Pollick, 2024.

While every precaution has been taken in the preparation of this book, the publisher assumes no responsibility for errors or omissions, or for damages resulting from the use of the information contained herein.

A WISE GEEK'S GUIDE TO EVERYTHING

First edition. September 6, 2024.

Copyright © 2024 Michael Pollick.

ISBN: 979-8227509864

Written by Michael Pollick.

Table of Contents

A Wise Geek's Guide To Everything

Michael Pollick

What Is A Cutaway?

A cutaway is a term that finds its roots in various fields, including film, architecture, and even literature. At its core, a cutaway serves as a visual or narrative device that provides insight into something that would otherwise remain hidden or obscured. In film, for instance, a cutaway shot is a brief transition away from the main action to show something else, often to provide context or to enhance the viewer's understanding of the scene. Imagine a tense moment in a thriller where the protagonist is cornered by an antagonist. A cutaway might shift the focus to a ticking clock or a close-up of a sweating brow, amplifying the suspense by highlighting the passage of time or the character's anxiety.

In architecture, a cutaway drawing reveals the internal structure of a building, allowing viewers to see how different elements interact. It's like peeling back the layers of an onion to expose the intricate details within. This technique is invaluable for architects and engineers, as it provides a clear visual representation of how spaces function and how materials come together.

In literature, the concept of a cutaway can be metaphorical. Writers often introduce a cutaway to delve into a character's backstory or to explore a theme that enriches the narrative. This can create a deeper connection between the reader and the characters, as it offers a glimpse into their motivations and histories.

Ultimately, a cutaway serves as a bridge, linking the known with the unknown, the visible with the invisible. It invites the audience to engage more deeply, encouraging them to look beyond the surface and appreciate the complexities that lie beneath. Whether in film, architecture, or literature, cutaways are essential tools for storytelling and understanding.

What Is A Keytar?

A keytar is an electronic musical instrument that combines the features of a keyboard and a guitar. It is essentially a synthesizer with a keyboard layout, but instead of being stationary like a traditional piano, it is designed to be worn like a guitar. This unique design allows musicians to move freely while performing, enabling them to engage with their audience in a way that a standard keyboardist might find challenging. The keytar typically has a lightweight body, a shoulder strap, and a keyboard that can range from 37 to 61 keys, depending on the model.

What sets the keytar apart from other instruments is its ability to produce a wide variety of sounds. It can emulate traditional instruments like pianos and strings, or it can create entirely new electronic sounds. Many keytars come equipped with MIDI capabilities, allowing them to control other electronic instruments or software, making them incredibly versatile in both live performances and studio recordings.

The origins of the keytar can be traced back to the 1980s, a decade known for its experimentation with electronic music. Early models were often bulky and limited in functionality, but as technology evolved, so did the design and capabilities of the keytar. Today, it is favored by many genres, from rock to pop, and has made a significant comeback in recent years, embraced by both nostalgic musicians and new artists alike.

In essence, the keytar is more than just a musical instrument; it's a bridge between the worlds of keyboard and guitar, offering musicians a dynamic way to express themselves. Whether in a concert hall or a small club, the keytar brings a unique flair that captivates audiences, making it a beloved choice for performers looking to add a little extra excitement to their music.

Who Owns The Song "Happy Birthday"?

The song "Happy Birthday to You" is one of the most recognizable melodies in the English-speaking world, often sung at birthday celebrations across the globe. Yet, for decades, the ownership of this simple tune has been shrouded in controversy and legal battles, raising the question: who actually owns the rights to "Happy Birthday"?

To understand the ownership of the song, we must first delve into its origins. The melody we know today was derived from a song called "Good Morning to All," which was composed by Patty Hill and her sister Mildred J. Hill in the late 19th century, around the 1890s. The Hill sisters were educators who wrote this song for young children, intending it to be a cheerful way to greet students at the start of the day. The lyrics of "Good Morning to All" were simple and straightforward, designed to be easily sung by children. However, as time went on, the melody became associated with birthday celebrations, and the lyrics were adapted to the now-familiar "Happy Birthday to You."

The transition from "Good Morning to All" to "Happy Birthday" is somewhat of a mystery, with various theories about how this transformation occurred. Some suggest that it was popularized in the early 20th century through informal gatherings and celebrations, while others point to the influence of early recordings and performances that helped solidify its place in birthday traditions. Regardless of how it happened, by the early 1900s, "Happy Birthday to You" was firmly entrenched in American culture.

But here's where it gets complicated. For many years, the song was considered to be in the public domain, meaning that anyone could use it without paying royalties. However, in the 1930s, a company called Warner/Chappell Music claimed ownership of the song and began charging fees for its use, particularly in films, television shows, and other commercial venues. This led to widespread confusion and frustration, as many believed that a song so ubiquitous and cherished should be free for all to enjoy.

The legal battle over "Happy Birthday" reached a peak in 2013 when a documentary filmmaker sought to use the song in his film without paying the licensing fee. He challenged the validity of Warner/Chappell's claim, arguing that the song should be in the public domain. The case attracted significant media attention and sparked a broader conversation about copyright laws and their implications for cultural works. Ultimately, a judge ruled in favor of the filmmaker, declaring that Warner/Chappell's claim to the song was not valid. This landmark decision effectively placed "Happy Birthday to You" back into the public domain, allowing anyone to sing or use the song without the fear of legal repercussions.

So, who owns "Happy Birthday" now? In a sense, it belongs to all of us. The melody, once the intellectual property of a music company, is now free for everyone to sing, celebrate, and enjoy. It is a collective cultural treasure, a melody that transcends age, nationality, and background. The song's return to the public domain is a victory for the spirit of creativity and community, reminding us that some things are meant to be shared and celebrated together.

In conclusion, the ownership of "Happy Birthday to You" reflects a larger narrative about copyright, creativity, and cultural heritage. It serves as a reminder that while individual creators deserve recognition and compensation for their work, certain cultural artifacts are meant to be part of the shared human experience. So, the next time you gather around a cake, surrounded by friends and family, and belt out that familiar tune, remember that it belongs to everyone. It is a song of joy, of celebration, and of togetherness, a melody that has woven itself into the fabric of our lives, free for all to sing.

What Are The Seven Modes Of Music?

Music, in its essence, is a universal language that transcends boundaries, cultures, and time. At the heart of this language lies a structure that guides its creation and interpretation. Among the fundamental components of music theory are the seven modes, each with its unique character and emotional resonance. Understanding these modes not only enriches our appreciation of music but also enhances our ability to create and perform. So, what are the seven modes of music, and how do they shape the soundscapes we encounter?

The first mode is the Ionian mode, which is essentially what we know as the major scale. It exudes a bright, happy sound, often associated with joy and celebration. The intervals that define the Ionian mode create a sense of resolution and completeness, making it a favorite for countless pop songs, anthems, and uplifting melodies. Its structure, built on the sequence of whole and half steps, offers a familiar and comforting foundation, inviting listeners to engage with its optimistic spirit.

Next comes the Dorian mode. This mode is often described as having a jazzy or soulful quality, striking a balance between brightness and melancholy. It is characterized by a minor third and a major sixth, which gives it a unique flavor. The Dorian mode is frequently used in jazz and blues, where its slightly darker undertones allow for emotional depth while still retaining a sense of hopefulness. It invites improvisation, making it a favorite among musicians looking to explore complex expressions of feeling.

The Phrygian mode follows, often evoking a sense of mystery or exoticism. With its flat second scale degree, the Phrygian mode carries an inherent tension that can create a feeling of suspense or drama. It's commonly found in flamenco music and can be heard in various forms of rock and metal, where its darker, more aggressive undertones lend themselves to powerful storytelling. The Phrygian mode challenges listeners to embrace complexity, often leading them down unexpected paths.

Then we have the Lydian mode, which is characterized by its raised fourth scale degree. This mode radiates a sense of brightness and wonder, often associated with a feeling of upliftment and creativity. The Lydian mode is frequently used in film scores and progressive rock, where its ethereal quality can transport listeners to otherworldly realms. It invites exploration and imagination, making it a favorite among composers and artists seeking to evoke feelings of transcendence.

The Mixolydian mode, on the other hand, is defined by its flat seventh scale degree. This mode has a dominant, bluesy quality that is prevalent in rock, country, and folk music. The Mixolydian mode brings a sense of resolution while retaining a playful tension, making it perfect for catchy melodies and sing-along choruses. It embodies a spirit of celebration and camaraderie, often found in songs that resonate with communal experiences.

Now, let's turn to the Aeolian mode, which is synonymous with the natural minor scale. This mode evokes a sense of introspection and melancholy, often exploring themes of loss and longing. Its structure allows for rich emotional storytelling, making it a staple in various genres, from classical to contemporary. The Aeolian mode invites listeners to reflect on their own experiences, creating a profound connection between the music and the emotions it elicits.

Finally, we arrive at the Locrian mode, the least common of the seven. With its diminished fifth, the Locrian mode carries an inherent instability that can evoke feelings of unease or tension. It is often used in experimental and avant-garde music, where its unpredictable nature allows for creative exploration. The Locrian mode challenges musicians to push boundaries, inviting them to explore the fringes of sound and emotion.

In conclusion, the seven modes of music—Ionian, Dorian, Phrygian, Lydian, Mixolydian, Aeolian, and Locrian—each offer a distinct palette of emotional colors and textures. They form the backbone of musical composition, guiding artists in their creative endeavors while inviting listeners to experience the rich tapestry of sound that defines our world. Understanding these modes deepens our connection to music, allowing us to appreciate the intricate beauty that lies within every note.

What Are Vinyl Records?

Vinyl records, often regarded as the quintessential medium for music enthusiasts, are more than just circular discs made of plastic; they are a bridge to the past, a tactile experience, and a celebration of sound. To understand what vinyl records are, we must delve into their history, construction, and the unique qualities that have led to their resurgence in popularity in recent years.

Historically, vinyl records emerged in the early 20th century, evolving from earlier formats like shellac records, which were brittle and prone to breakage. The introduction of polyvinyl chloride, or PVC, in the late 1940s marked a significant turning point. This new material was not only more durable but also allowed for better sound quality. The 33 1/3 RPM long-playing record, or LP, became the standard format, capable of holding multiple tracks on each side, which was revolutionary at the time. The 45 RPM single also gained popularity, offering a more concise listening experience. These formats quickly became the backbone of the music industry, with record labels producing a vast array of genres, from jazz to rock to classical.

But what exactly are these records made of? At their core, vinyl records consist of a flat disc with grooves etched into their surface. These grooves are not merely decorative; they are the physical representation of sound waves. When a record spins on a turntable, a needle, or stylus, follows these grooves, translating the physical undulations into electrical signals. These signals are then amplified and transformed back into sound waves, allowing listeners to experience music as it was intended. The craftsmanship involved in creating a vinyl record is intricate. From mastering the audio to cutting the master disc and pressing the final product, each step requires precision and expertise.

One of the defining characteristics of vinyl records is their analog nature. Unlike digital formats, which convert sound into binary code, vinyl captures the continuous waveforms of sound. This analog quality is often cited as a reason for the warmer, richer sound that many audiophiles prefer. Vinyl records can convey subtleties in music that digital formats may overlook, creating a more immersive listening experience. The dynamic range, the depth of sound, and even the occasional pops and crackles that come with a well-loved record add to its charm, creating a connection between the listener and the music that is often described as intimate.

Moreover, the physicality of vinyl records contributes to their allure. Unlike streaming music, which can feel ephemeral and intangible, vinyl demands a more engaged listening experience. The act of selecting a record, carefully placing it on the turntable, and gently lowering the needle becomes a ritual. The large, visually striking album artwork provides a canvas for artistic expression, allowing musicians to convey their vision in ways that digital formats cannot. Collecting vinyl records has become a hobby for many, with enthusiasts hunting for rare pressings, exploring record stores, and sharing their finds with fellow aficionados.

In recent years, vinyl has made a remarkable comeback, defying the digital age's dominance. Sales have surged, with vinyl records outselling CDs in some markets for the first time in decades. This resurgence can be attributed to a growing appreciation for the tactile, analog experience, as well as a desire for authenticity in an increasingly digital world. Many contemporary artists are releasing their music on vinyl, recognizing its cultural significance and the loyal fan base that cherishes it.

In conclusion, vinyl records are not merely relics of a bygone era; they are a vibrant part of music culture that continues to captivate new generations. They represent a unique blend of artistry, craftsmanship, and nostalgia, inviting listeners to engage with music in a way that is both personal and profound. As we continue to navigate the complexities of modern technology, vinyl records stand as a testament to the enduring power of music and the timeless joy of listening.

What Is Sundowners' Syndrome?

Sundowners' Syndrome, often referred to as sundowning, is a phenomenon typically associated with older adults, particularly those suffering from Alzheimer's disease or other forms of dementia. It manifests as increased confusion, agitation, and anxiety during the late afternoon and evening hours. The exact cause of sundowning remains unclear, but it is believed to be linked to changes in the body's internal clock, or circadian rhythms, which can be disrupted in individuals with cognitive impairments.

As the sun sets, the decrease in natural light can lead to heightened feelings of disorientation. This is compounded by fatigue that accumulates throughout the day, as well as the potential for shadows and dim lighting to create an unsettling environment. In these moments, familiar surroundings may appear unfamiliar, leading to distress and confusion.

Symptoms of sundowning can vary widely among individuals. Some may exhibit restlessness or wandering behavior, while others might become irritable or exhibit mood swings. It's not uncommon for caregivers to witness a dramatic shift in behavior as the day transitions into night, which can be particularly challenging for both the individual and their loved ones.

Managing sundowners' syndrome often involves creating a calming evening routine. Strategies may include maintaining consistent daily schedules, ensuring adequate exposure to natural light during the day, and minimizing noise and distractions in the evening. Some caregivers find that engaging individuals in soothing activities, such as listening to music or engaging in light conversation, can help ease the transition into nighttime.

Understanding sundowners' syndrome is crucial for providing compassionate care and support. By recognizing the signs and implementing effective strategies, caregivers can help individuals navigate this challenging aspect of dementia, ultimately improving their quality of life and fostering a sense of security during the twilight hours.

What Is A Cover Band?

A cover band is a musical group that performs songs originally created by other artists, rather than composing their own original music. This concept has been around for decades, rooted deeply in the fabric of popular music culture. Cover bands can vary widely in their approach, style, and purpose. Some may focus on faithfully recreating the sound and arrangements of the original artists, while others might take creative liberties, reinterpreting songs in unique ways. This flexibility allows cover bands to appeal to a diverse audience, catering to different tastes and preferences.

At its core, the idea of a cover band is about homage. It's a way for musicians to celebrate the music that has influenced them, to pay tribute to the artists they admire, and to connect with fans of those original songs. Cover bands often perform in various settings, from local bars and clubs to larger festivals and events. They provide an accessible form of entertainment, allowing audiences to enjoy familiar tunes in a live setting. For many, the experience of hearing a favorite song performed live is a thrill that can evoke powerful memories and emotions.

Cover bands are not just about nostalgia; they also serve a practical purpose in the music industry. For many aspiring musicians, starting as a cover band is a stepping stone. It allows them to hone their skills, learn the intricacies of performance, and build a following. By playing well-known songs, they can attract crowds and gain experience in front of live audiences without the pressure of needing to create original material right away. This can be particularly beneficial for new musicians who are still developing their unique sound and stage presence.

Moreover, cover bands can introduce audiences to music they might not have encountered otherwise. A skilled band might perform a deep cut from an artist's catalog or cover a lesser-known song that resonates with listeners. This can spark interest in the original artist's work, leading fans to explore their discography and discover new favorites. In this way, cover bands act as a bridge, connecting different generations of music lovers and fostering appreciation for a wide range of musical styles.

The diversity of cover bands is another fascinating aspect of this phenomenon. Some bands specialize in a specific genre, like classic rock, pop, or country, while others might blend various styles, creating unique mashups that surprise and delight audiences. Tribute bands take this concept even further, dedicating themselves to replicating the music and performance style of a particular artist or band. These tribute acts often go to great lengths to mimic not just the sound but also the look and feel of the original performers, creating an immersive experience for fans.

However, the world of cover bands is not without its controversies. Some argue that cover bands can detract from the original artists' work, overshadowing their creativity and innovation. Others feel that performing covers diminishes a musician's credibility and artistic integrity. Yet, many artists recognize the value of cover bands, understanding that their music can live on through reinterpretation. Iconic figures like Bruce Springsteen and the Rolling Stones have often acknowledged the joy of hearing their songs covered by other musicians, seeing it as a testament to their impact on the music scene.

In conclusion, cover bands play a multifaceted role in the music landscape. They are entertainers, educators, and even cultural ambassadors, bridging gaps between generations and genres. They allow musicians to grow and develop while providing audiences with the joy of live music. Whether they're recreating the sounds of the past or putting their own spin on beloved classics, cover bands are an essential part of the musical tapestry, reminding us all of the power of song to connect us, inspire us, and bring us together in celebration of the art form we love.

What Is A Stentorian Voice?

A stentorian voice is one that commands attention, characterized by its loud, powerful, and resonant quality. The term itself derives from the name of Stentor, a herald in Greek mythology, who was said to have a voice as loud as that of fifty men combined. This concept of a stentorian voice transcends mere volume; it embodies a certain gravitas and authority that can captivate an audience. Such a voice is often associated with public speakers, leaders, and performers who possess the ability to project their voice in a way that not only fills a room but also resonates with listeners on an emotional level.

To understand what constitutes a stentorian voice, one must consider several key attributes. First, there is the aspect of projection. A stentorian voice is not just loud; it is clear and distinct, cutting through background noise with ease. This clarity allows the speaker to convey their message effectively, ensuring that every word is heard and understood. Moreover, a stentorian voice often carries a rich tonal quality, which adds depth and warmth, making the delivery more engaging.

Another important characteristic is the ability to modulate. A true stentorian voice can shift in volume and intensity, creating a dynamic listening experience. This modulation helps to emphasize key points and maintain the audience's interest, preventing the delivery from becoming monotonous. Additionally, a stentorian voice often conveys confidence and authority, traits that can inspire trust and respect from listeners.

In various contexts, whether in a classroom, a theater, or a political rally, the power of a stentorian voice can be transformative. It can rally crowds, educate minds, and even soothe fears. Ultimately, a stentorian voice is not merely about being loud; it is about the ability to communicate effectively and leave a lasting impact.

What Are Compression Shorts?

Compression shorts are a specialized type of athletic wear designed to provide support and improve performance during physical activities. They are typically made from a blend of spandex, nylon, or polyester, which allows them to fit snugly against the body. This tight fit serves several key purposes. Firstly, compression shorts help to increase blood circulation in the muscles, which can enhance oxygen delivery and reduce fatigue during exercise. This is particularly beneficial for athletes engaging in high-intensity workouts or endurance sports, as improved circulation can lead to better overall performance.

Another significant advantage of compression shorts is their ability to minimize muscle vibration. When you run or engage in high-impact activities, your muscles experience a certain amount of jostling, which can lead to soreness and fatigue. Compression shorts help to stabilize the muscles, reducing this vibration and potentially decreasing the risk of injury. This is especially crucial for runners, cyclists, and team sport athletes who put their bodies through repetitive motions.

Moreover, compression shorts can aid in recovery after workouts. Wearing them post-exercise can help to reduce muscle soreness and speed up the recovery process by promoting better blood flow and reducing lactic acid buildup. Many athletes incorporate them into their post-workout routine for this reason.

In addition to their functional benefits, compression shorts are often designed with moisture-wicking properties, keeping the wearer dry and comfortable during intense workouts. They come in various lengths and styles, catering to different preferences and needs. Overall, compression shorts have become a staple in athletic wardrobes, valued for their ability to enhance performance, support recovery, and provide comfort during physical activities. Whether you're a seasoned athlete or just starting your fitness journey, investing in a good pair of compression shorts can be a game changer.

What Is A Scottish Shower?

A Scottish shower is not just a whimsical phrase; it's a term that captures the essence of Scotland's unpredictable weather. Imagine stepping outside, and within moments, the sun is shining brightly, only to be interrupted by a sudden downpour. This phenomenon is an apt metaphor for the Scottish climate, where it's not uncommon to experience all four seasons in a single day. The term itself is often used to describe a brief but intense rain shower, typically accompanied by gusty winds and a hint of sunshine peeking through the clouds.

The origins of this term can be traced back to the rugged landscapes and ever-changing weather patterns of Scotland. The country is known for its dramatic scenery, from the rolling hills of the Highlands to the serene lochs, and the weather plays a crucial role in shaping this environment. The Scottish shower is a reminder of the region's wild beauty and the resilience of its people, who have learned to embrace the rain as part of their daily lives.

Culturally, the Scottish shower has become a point of humor and pride. Locals often joke about the need to carry an umbrella at all times, as the weather can shift in an instant. It's a shared experience that fosters camaraderie among Scots, who understand that a sunny moment can quickly turn into a soaking wet one.

In essence, a Scottish shower is more than just rain; it's a reflection of the unpredictable nature of life itself. It teaches us to appreciate the fleeting moments of sunshine amidst the storms, to find joy in the unexpected, and to adapt to whatever comes our way. So, the next time you find yourself caught in a downpour, remember that you're experiencing a little piece of Scotland.

What Is A Bland Diet?

A bland diet is often recommended for individuals experiencing digestive issues, recovering from surgery, or facing certain medical conditions. Essentially, it consists of foods that are gentle on the stomach and easy to digest. The primary goal is to minimize irritation to the gastrointestinal tract while providing essential nutrients. Typically, this diet includes plain foods that are low in fiber, fat, and spices. Think of things like white rice, applesauce, bananas, toast—often referred to as the "BRAT" diet, which stands for bananas, rice, applesauce, and toast. These foods are less likely to cause discomfort or exacerbate symptoms like nausea, diarrhea, or heartburn.

When considering a bland diet, it's crucial to avoid items that are spicy, fatty, or high in fiber. This means steering clear of fried foods, rich sauces, and raw fruits or vegetables, which may lead to bloating or gas. Instead, the focus is on well-cooked, soft foods that are easy to chew and swallow. For proteins, options like boiled chicken, eggs, or fish can be included, while dairy products should be consumed cautiously, as they might not sit well with everyone.

While a bland diet can be beneficial in the short term, it's important to recognize that it's not meant for long-term adherence. Nutritionally, it can be quite limiting, lacking in variety and essential vitamins and minerals. Therefore, once symptoms improve, individuals are usually encouraged to gradually reintroduce a wider range of foods to ensure a balanced diet. In summary, a bland diet serves as a temporary measure, providing comfort and relief for those in need while paving the way for a return to a more diverse and nutritious eating pattern.

What Is Mountain Dew Mouth?

Mountain Dew Mouth, a term that might sound whimsical but carries serious implications, refers to a condition primarily associated with excessive consumption of sugary soft drinks, particularly Mountain Dew. This phenomenon is most commonly observed in certain demographics, often linked to regions where the beverage is a staple, especially among young people and those with limited access to dental care. The condition manifests as severe dental decay, characterized by a striking pattern of cavities, erosion, and sometimes even tooth loss.

The root of the problem lies in the high sugar content and acidity of these beverages. Mountain Dew, for instance, contains citric acid and phosphoric acid, which can erode tooth enamel, making teeth more susceptible to decay. When consumed in large quantities, the sugar feeds bacteria in the mouth, creating an environment ripe for cavities. The term "Mountain Dew Mouth" encapsulates not just the physical deterioration of dental health but also the cultural factors that contribute to it.

In many cases, the individuals affected may not have adequate access to dental education or resources, leading to a cycle of neglect regarding oral hygiene. The allure of these sugary drinks, often marketed in vibrant colors and catchy slogans, can overshadow the long-term consequences of their consumption.

Moreover, the social implications are significant. Poor dental health can affect self-esteem, social interactions, and even employment opportunities. It's a stark reminder of how dietary choices can have profound effects on overall health, particularly in communities where sugary drinks are a common fixture. Awareness and education are crucial in combating this condition, encouraging healthier choices, and fostering better dental habits among vulnerable populations. Understanding Mountain Dew Mouth is not just about dental health; it's about addressing broader issues of nutrition, access, and education in our society.

What Is A Notary Public?

A notary public is, at first glance, just a person with a stamp, a signature, and a few official-looking documents. But delve a little deeper, and you'll find a role steeped in trust, integrity, and the preservation of truth. In a world where everything is digitized, where authenticity can feel like a fleeting concept, a notary stands as a guardian of the written word. They are the gatekeepers of legality, ensuring that agreements are not just words on paper but binding commitments.

Imagine a couple, excitedly signing their first mortgage agreement. They've spent months searching, dreaming, and finally, they're here, ready to make it official. The notary enters, not just as a facilitator but as a witness to their dreams. They check IDs, verify identities, and make sure that both parties are entering this contract willingly, free from coercion. It's a small act, but it carries immense weight.

Then there are the businesses, the entrepreneurs who need contracts validated, the power of attorney documents that dictate futures, and the wills that carry legacies. A notary public ensures that these documents hold up in a court of law, that they don't crumble under scrutiny. They're trained to spot forgeries, to recognize when something feels off, to ask the right questions.

In essence, a notary public embodies a commitment to honesty. They are the silent witnesses to life's most significant moments, ensuring that when we put pen to paper, we do so with the understanding that our words matter. In a society that often feels chaotic, the notary provides a sense of order, a reminder that some things are still bound by trust and authenticity. So, the next time you see that stamp, remember: it's not just ink; it's a promise.

What Is The Wonderlic Personnel Test?

The Wonderlic Personnel Test is a cognitive ability assessment that has been used for decades to evaluate the intellectual capacity of individuals, particularly in a workplace setting. Developed in 1934 by Eldon Wonderlic, a psychologist and educator, the test was originally created as a tool to help employers make more informed hiring decisions. It consists of 50 multiple-choice questions that must be answered within a 12-minute time limit, covering a variety of topics such as math, vocabulary, and reasoning. The test is designed to measure general cognitive ability, which is often associated with job performance and the ability to learn new skills.

One of the key features of the Wonderlic test is its emphasis on speed and accuracy. The time constraint adds a layer of pressure that simulates real-world scenarios where quick thinking and problem-solving are essential. This aspect of the test can be both a strength and a weakness. On one hand, it helps employers identify candidates who can think on their feet and perform well under stress. On the other hand, the limited time can disadvantage individuals who may be capable of deep analytical thinking but require more time to process information.

The scoring of the Wonderlic test is straightforward. Each correct answer earns one point, and the total score can range from 0 to 50. The average score for most job applicants is around 20, which corresponds to an IQ of approximately 100. However, the interpretation of scores can vary significantly depending on the specific job or industry. For example, positions that require advanced problem-solving skills, such as engineering or software development, may expect higher scores, while roles that focus more on manual labor may not place as much emphasis on cognitive testing.

Critics of the Wonderlic test argue that it can be biased against certain demographic groups, particularly those from lower socioeconomic backgrounds or with less access to quality education. They contend that a single test score cannot accurately reflect an individual's potential or capabilities. Additionally, there are concerns about the test's reliance on cognitive ability as a predictor of job performance, as many other factors, such as emotional intelligence, interpersonal skills, and work ethic, also play crucial roles in an employee's success.

Despite these criticisms, the Wonderlic test remains popular among employers, especially in industries where quick decision-making and problem-solving are paramount. Companies like Google, NFL teams, and various organizations in the tech sector have used the test as part of their hiring process. The appeal lies in its simplicity and the ability to quickly filter candidates based on cognitive ability. Some organizations even use the results to tailor training and development programs for new hires, aligning their strengths and weaknesses with the demands of the job.

In recent years, the test has also been adapted for various contexts beyond traditional employment. For instance, some educational institutions use modified versions of the Wonderlic to assess students' readiness for certain programs or courses. This expansion of the test's application reflects a growing recognition of the importance of cognitive assessment in diverse settings.

Ultimately, the Wonderlic Personnel Test serves as a tool that can provide valuable insights into an individual's cognitive abilities. However, it is essential for employers to use the test as just one component of a comprehensive evaluation process. Combining test results with interviews, reference checks, and other assessment methods can lead to more holistic hiring decisions. In a world where talent is often the most significant competitive advantage, understanding the strengths and limitations of tools like the Wonderlic test is crucial for fostering a diverse and capable workforce.

What Is A White Collar Job?

When we think about jobs, we often visualize the traditional blue-collar worker, perhaps someone in a factory or on a construction site, engaging in manual labor. However, there's another category of employment that has come to dominate the modern workforce: the white-collar job. But what exactly is a white-collar job? To answer this question, we need to delve into the characteristics, responsibilities, and societal implications of this type of work.

White-collar jobs are typically characterized by their focus on office-based tasks, as opposed to manual labor. The term itself was popularized in the early 20th century, largely attributed to sociologist Edward S. M. W. W. L. Wright, who used it to describe workers who wore white dress shirts and worked in an office environment. These jobs are often associated with professional, managerial, or administrative roles, and they usually require a certain level of education, training, or specialized skills. In contrast to blue-collar jobs, which often emphasize physical strength and skill, white-collar jobs rely on mental acuity, analytical abilities, and interpersonal skills.

In terms of industries, white-collar jobs can be found across a wide spectrum. They exist in finance, healthcare, technology, education, and more. Think of accountants, engineers, marketing specialists, human resource managers, and software developers. Each of these roles requires a different skill set, but they share common traits: they often involve problem-solving, critical thinking, and communication. Employees in these positions typically spend their workdays in offices, collaborating with colleagues, attending meetings, and utilizing technology to perform their tasks.

One of the defining features of white-collar jobs is the level of compensation they offer. Generally, these positions tend to provide higher salaries than blue-collar jobs. The disparity in pay is often due to the educational requirements and the specialized skills needed for many white-collar roles. For example, a medical doctor, a lawyer, or a software engineer usually requires extensive education and training, which justifies their higher earning potential. However, it's important to note that not all white-collar jobs are high-paying; some administrative roles may offer modest salaries, but they still fall under the white-collar umbrella.

Job security and benefits are also significant aspects of white-collar employment. Many white-collar jobs come with benefits such as health insurance, retirement plans, and paid time off, making them attractive to workers seeking stability and work-life balance. Additionally, the nature of these jobs often allows for greater flexibility, with options for remote work or flexible hours becoming increasingly common, especially in the wake of the COVID-19 pandemic. This shift has transformed the landscape of white-collar work, allowing employees to maintain productivity while enjoying a more adaptable work environment.

However, it's essential to recognize that white-collar jobs are not without their challenges. The pressure to perform, meet deadlines, and achieve targets can lead to stress and burnout. The competitive nature of many industries can also create a high-stakes atmosphere where job security is never guaranteed. Moreover, the rise of automation and artificial intelligence poses a potential threat to certain white-collar roles, raising questions about the future of work in this sector.

In conclusion, a white-collar job is defined by its office-based environment, focus on professional or administrative tasks, and reliance on specialized skills. These positions span various industries and typically offer higher salaries and benefits compared to blue-collar jobs. While they come with their own set of challenges, including stress and job security concerns, white-collar jobs continue to play a vital role in our economy and society. As the workforce evolves, understanding the nuances of white-collar employment becomes crucial for navigating the complexities of the modern job market. Whether one is entering the workforce or considering a career change, recognizing the significance and implications of white-collar jobs can provide valuable insights into the opportunities that lie ahead.

What Is The Hedonic Treadmill?

The hedonic treadmill, a concept rooted in psychology and economics, describes the human tendency to quickly return to a relatively stable level of happiness despite significant positive or negative events or life changes. Imagine this: you've just received a promotion at work, a significant raise, and you're filled with elation. You revel in the moment, basking in the warmth of your achievement, but as days turn into weeks, that joy begins to fade. The initial thrill, that euphoric high, slowly dissipates, and soon you find yourself back at your baseline level of happiness. This phenomenon is what we call the hedonic treadmill.

The term was coined by psychologists Brickman and Campbell in the 1970s, who conducted studies that revealed how people generally adapt to both positive and negative changes in their lives. They likened this adaptation to a treadmill—no matter how fast you run or how hard you try to elevate your happiness, you're ultimately stuck in the same place. This idea is particularly relevant in our consumer-driven society, where the pursuit of happiness often hinges on acquiring more: more money, more possessions, more experiences. Yet, the hedonic treadmill suggests that these acquisitions may provide only temporary satisfaction.

Consider the case of lottery winners. Studies show that while winning a substantial amount of money can lead to a spike in happiness, most winners eventually return to their previous level of contentment. The initial excitement of newfound wealth fades, and they find themselves seeking out new sources of joy, often leading them back to the very same emotional state they experienced before the windfall. Conversely, those who experience significant hardships, like losing a job or going through a divorce, also tend to return to their baseline happiness over time. While these events may cause profound distress initially, people have an incredible capacity for resilience.

This cycle of adaptation can be explained by the concept of relative deprivation. People often measure their happiness in relation to others. If you live in a neighborhood where everyone drives luxury cars, your happiness might dip if you're driving an older model. However, if you move to a different area where the standard of living is lower, suddenly your car doesn't seem so bad. This constant comparison fuels the treadmill effect, as we continuously seek to elevate our status or possessions to keep up with those around us.

The implications of the hedonic treadmill stretch far beyond personal happiness. They affect broader societal issues as well. The relentless pursuit of wealth and material goods can lead to a cycle of overconsumption and environmental degradation. As we chase after fleeting moments of joy, we often overlook the more sustainable sources of happiness that lie in relationships, experiences, and personal growth.

So, what can one do to break free from the confines of the hedonic treadmill? Research suggests that cultivating gratitude, mindfulness, and focusing on experiences rather than possessions can help. When we appreciate what we have, rather than constantly yearning for more, we can find deeper, more lasting satisfaction. Engaging in meaningful relationships and fostering connections with others can also provide a sense of fulfillment that transcends the temporary highs of material gains.

Ultimately, the hedonic treadmill serves as a reminder of the complexities of human emotion and the pursuit of happiness. It challenges us to reconsider our definitions of success and fulfillment. Instead of chasing after the next big thing, perhaps we should pause and reflect on the simple joys that life offers—moments spent with loved ones, the beauty of nature, or the satisfaction of personal achievement that doesn't rely on external validation. In doing so, we may discover that true happiness isn't about the relentless chase, but rather the appreciation of the present moment and the connections we forge along the way.

What Is A Letter Of Intent?

A letter of intent is a formal document that outlines the intentions of one party to engage in a specific action, often in a business or academic context. It serves as a preliminary agreement, signaling a commitment to negotiate terms and conditions that will govern a future relationship or transaction. While it is not legally binding in the same way a contract is, it establishes a framework for the parties involved, detailing the main points of agreement and the objectives they aim to achieve.

In academia, a letter of intent is commonly used by applicants applying for graduate programs or fellowships. It expresses the applicant's goals, research interests, and reasons for choosing a particular program or institution. This document allows candidates to showcase their qualifications and aspirations, giving admissions committees insight into their motivations and how they align with the program's mission. It can be a critical component of the application process, helping applicants stand out in a competitive field.

In the business world, a letter of intent often precedes significant transactions, such as mergers, acquisitions, or partnerships. It outlines the basic terms of the deal, including price, structure, and timeline, while also addressing confidentiality and exclusivity agreements. By laying out these intentions, the letter helps to prevent misunderstandings and ensures that both parties are on the same page before moving forward with more detailed negotiations.

Ultimately, a letter of intent is a vital tool for communication, clarifying the intentions of the parties involved and paving the way for future collaboration. It encapsulates hopes, plans, and mutual interests, serving as a stepping stone toward more formal agreements that will solidify the relationship and the path forward. Understanding its purpose and significance can greatly enhance one's ability to navigate professional and academic landscapes effectively.

What Is A Trademark?

A trademark is essentially a symbol, word, or phrase that is legally registered or established by use as representing a company or product. It serves as a distinctive sign that identifies and differentiates the source of goods or services from those of others. Trademarks can take many forms, including logos, brand names, slogans, and even sounds or colors. Think of the iconic swoosh of Nike or the golden arches of McDonald's; these are not just images; they are powerful representations of the brands they belong to, instilling an immediate association in the minds of consumers.

The purpose of a trademark is to protect the brand identity and ensure that consumers can easily recognize and trust the products or services associated with it. This protection is crucial in a marketplace flooded with options, where consumers rely on trademarks to make informed purchasing decisions. When a customer sees a trademark, they are not just seeing a logo; they are seeing a promise of quality, reliability, and consistency. Trademarks help to prevent confusion among consumers and protect them from inferior or counterfeit products.

To gain trademark protection, a company must register its trademark with the appropriate government authority, such as the United States Patent and Trademark Office (USPTO) in the United States. However, it is important to note that even unregistered trademarks can have some level of protection under common law, provided they have been used in commerce and have acquired distinctiveness. The registration process involves several steps, including submitting an application that outlines the trademark, its intended use, and the goods or services it will represent. The trademark must then undergo a review process to ensure it does not conflict with existing trademarks and meets the necessary criteria for registration.

Once registered, a trademark grants the owner exclusive rights to use the mark in connection with the specified goods or services. This exclusivity is crucial because it allows the trademark owner to take legal action against anyone who attempts to use a similar mark that could cause confusion in the marketplace. Infringement can lead to significant legal battles, as companies work to protect their intellectual property and maintain their brand integrity.

Trademarks are not just limited to tangible products; they can also apply to services. Service marks are similar to trademarks but specifically protect the branding of services rather than goods. For example, the name of a restaurant or a consulting firm can be protected under service mark law. The significance of this protection extends beyond mere branding; it fosters consumer loyalty and trust. When a consumer chooses a service based on its recognizable mark, they are often making a decision rooted in familiarity and past experiences.

Moreover, trademarks can be renewed indefinitely as long as they are being used in commerce and the renewal fees are paid. This longevity allows brands to build a legacy over time. Think about Coca-Cola; its trademark has been around for over a century, and it continues to be one of the most recognized brands in the world. The value of a trademark can also increase as a brand grows, making it a valuable asset for businesses.

While trademarks are essential for businesses, they also play a role in promoting fair competition. By protecting brand identities, trademarks encourage innovation and quality. Companies are motivated to invest in their products and services, knowing that their unique identifiers are safeguarded from imitation. This dynamic fosters a competitive marketplace where businesses strive to improve and differentiate themselves.

In conclusion, a trademark is much more than a simple logo or name; it is a fundamental aspect of branding that carries significant legal protections and economic value. It represents the relationship between a company and its consumers, ensuring that the quality and identity of products and services remain intact. Understanding trademarks is vital for anyone navigating the business landscape, as they are integral to establishing and maintaining a successful brand.

What Is A Conflict Of Interest?

A conflict of interest arises when an individual or organization has multiple interests, one of which could potentially corrupt the motivation for an act in another interest. This situation can create a dilemma, as the conflicting interests may lead to a compromise in judgment, integrity, or the ability to act in the best interest of others. It's essential to understand that conflicts of interest can manifest in various settings, including business, law, healthcare, and even personal relationships.

In a business context, imagine a scenario where a company executive is in charge of deciding which vendor to award a lucrative contract. If this executive has a personal relationship with one of the vendors, or perhaps even holds shares in that vendor's company, a conflict of interest arises. The executive's personal financial interests might cloud their judgment, leading them to favor the vendor that benefits them personally rather than the one that would provide the best service or value to the company. This situation is not just unethical; it can also lead to legal ramifications and damage the company's reputation.

In the legal field, conflicts of interest are particularly critical. Lawyers are required to uphold the highest ethical standards, and a conflict of interest can undermine the trust that clients place in their legal representatives. For example, if a lawyer represents two clients with opposing interests in the same case, they face an ethical quandary. They may struggle to advocate effectively for both clients, as doing so could mean compromising the interests of one to serve the other.

Legal ethics often mandate that lawyers disclose any potential conflicts to their clients and seek their informed consent. If a conflict cannot be resolved, the lawyer must withdraw from representing one of the parties involved to maintain professional integrity.

Healthcare is another domain where conflicts of interest can have serious implications. Physicians, for instance, may face conflicts when they receive incentives from pharmaceutical companies for prescribing certain medications. This situation raises questions about whether the physician's recommendations are genuinely in the best interest of the patient or influenced by financial gain. Transparency in these relationships is crucial; healthcare professionals are often required to disclose any financial ties to pharmaceutical companies or medical device manufacturers to ensure that patients can make informed decisions about their care.

Furthermore, conflicts of interest can extend into personal relationships. Consider a situation where a person is tasked with making a decision that affects their family member's career. If that individual has a vested interest in the outcome—say, they stand to gain financially or emotionally from a particular decision—this can lead to biased choices that may not serve the broader community or organization involved. The challenge lies in balancing personal loyalties with the responsibility to act fairly and justly toward others.

To mitigate the risks associated with conflicts of interest, many organizations implement policies and procedures designed to identify and manage these situations. This might include mandatory disclosures, ethics training, and establishing clear guidelines on how to handle potential conflicts. Transparency is a vital component in fostering trust, whether in business, law, healthcare, or personal relationships. When individuals are open about their interests and potential conflicts, it allows for accountability and a chance to address any ethical concerns before they escalate into more significant issues.

In conclusion, understanding what constitutes a conflict of interest is essential for maintaining ethical standards across various fields. It requires vigilance, transparency, and a commitment to prioritizing the interests of others over personal gain. By recognizing and addressing conflicts of interest proactively, individuals and organizations can uphold integrity and trust, ensuring that their decisions are guided by fairness and ethical considerations. The challenge lies not only in identifying these conflicts but also in navigating them with a moral compass that prioritizes the greater good.

What Is Invasion Of Privacy?

Invasion of privacy is a concept that resonates deeply in our increasingly interconnected world, where personal boundaries seem to blur more with each passing day. At its core, invasion of privacy refers to the violation of an individual's right to keep their personal life, information, and communications private. This violation can manifest in various forms, ranging from unauthorized surveillance and data breaches to intrusive media coverage and even the casual sharing of personal information without consent. The implications of such invasions are profound, affecting not only the individuals involved but also the broader fabric of society.

To understand invasion of privacy fully, one must first acknowledge the different dimensions it encompasses. One of the most commonly recognized forms is the unauthorized collection of personal data. In our digital age, where social media platforms, online services, and mobile applications collect vast amounts of information about users, the line between acceptable data gathering and invasion of privacy becomes increasingly blurred. Companies often justify their data collection practices by claiming they enhance user experience or provide personalized services. However, when individuals are unaware of how their data is being used or shared, it raises ethical questions about consent and transparency. The Cambridge Analytica scandal, for example, highlighted how personal data could be exploited for political gain without the explicit consent of users, leaving many feeling betrayed and violated.

Another significant aspect of invasion of privacy is surveillance. In an era where technology enables constant monitoring, both by the state and private entities, the right to privacy is under siege. Governments may argue that surveillance is necessary for national security or crime prevention, but this often comes at the cost of individual freedoms. The revelations about the National Security Agency's extensive surveillance programs revealed a stark reality: millions of individuals had their communications monitored without their knowledge. This raises the question of how much privacy individuals are willing to sacrifice for the sake of security and whether the balance has tipped too far in favor of surveillance.

Moreover, invasion of privacy is not limited to digital realms; it also extends to physical spaces. Paparazzi culture, for instance, exemplifies how the relentless pursuit of celebrities often leads to egregious violations of their privacy. The public's insatiable curiosity about the lives of the famous can drive photographers to trespass on private property or invade personal moments, all in the name of entertainment. This raises ethical concerns about the boundaries of public interest versus individual rights. While celebrities may be public figures, they are still entitled to a degree of privacy, and the consequences of relentless intrusion can be devastating, leading to mental health struggles and even tragic outcomes.

Furthermore, the concept of invasion of privacy is evolving in response to societal changes. The rise of artificial intelligence and machine learning has introduced new challenges. Algorithms can analyze personal data to predict behaviors, preferences, and even vulnerabilities. This not only raises concerns about consent but also about the potential for discrimination and manipulation. When individuals are subjected to targeted advertising or content based on their private information, it can create an echo chamber that limits exposure to diverse viewpoints and reinforces existing biases.

In conclusion, invasion of privacy is a multifaceted issue that demands careful consideration as we navigate the complexities of modern life. It encompasses unauthorized data collection, surveillance, media intrusion, and the implications of emerging technologies. As individuals, we must advocate for our right to privacy and demand transparency from those who collect and utilize our personal information. Society as a whole must grapple with the ethical implications of these invasions and strive to strike a balance between the benefits of technology and the fundamental rights of individuals. Ultimately, the preservation of privacy is not merely a personal concern; it is a cornerstone of a free and democratic society, one that deserves our unwavering commitment and vigilance.

What Is Defamation Of Character?

Defamation of character is a legal term that refers to the act of damaging someone's reputation through false statements. It encompasses two main categories: libel and slander. Libel pertains to written or published defamatory statements, while slander refers to spoken defamatory remarks. To understand defamation of character fully, it's essential to break down its components and implications.

At its core, defamation involves a false statement presented as a fact. This is crucial because truth is a complete defense against defamation claims. If a statement can be proven true, no matter how damaging, it typically does not constitute defamation. The essence of defamation is that the statement must be untrue and harmful. This means that the person making the statement has to have acted negligently, or in some cases, with actual malice, especially if the individual being defamed is a public figure.

Public figures, including celebrities and politicians, have a higher burden to prove defamation. They must show that the false statement was made with actual malice, meaning the person knew the statement was false or acted with reckless disregard for the truth. This higher standard exists to encourage open discourse and criticism in society, recognizing that public figures have voluntarily stepped into the spotlight and should be subject to scrutiny.

On the other hand, private individuals have more protection. They only need to prove that the statement was made negligently. This distinction is significant because it underscores the balance between free speech and protecting individuals from falsehoods that could harm their reputation. The law recognizes that private individuals have a greater interest in safeguarding their reputation, as they may not have the same platform to defend themselves as public figures.

The impact of defamation can be profound. A false statement can lead to loss of employment, damaged relationships, and emotional distress. The repercussions can extend beyond the individual to affect families and communities, creating a ripple effect of harm. In today's digital age, the potential for defamation has increased dramatically. Social media platforms allow for rapid dissemination of information, making it easier for false statements to spread quickly and widely. Once a damaging statement is out in the public domain, it can be challenging to contain or retract, leading to long-lasting consequences.

To pursue a defamation claim, the affected party must demonstrate several elements. First, there must be a false statement presented as a fact. Second, the statement must be published or communicated to a third party. Third, it must cause harm to the reputation of the individual. Lastly, depending on whether the person is a public or private figure, the required level of fault must be established, either negligence or actual malice.

Defamation laws vary by jurisdiction, reflecting different societal values and legal principles. In some countries, defamation is treated as a criminal offense, while in others, it is primarily a civil matter. The penalties for defamation can include monetary damages, which aim to compensate the victim for the harm suffered. In some cases, courts may also issue injunctions to prevent further dissemination of the defamatory statements.

Defamation of character is not merely a legal issue; it's a societal concern that raises questions about ethics, accountability, and the responsibility that comes with freedom of expression. As we navigate an increasingly interconnected world, the lines between opinion and fact can blur, making it essential for individuals to be mindful of the words they choose. The balance between protecting one's reputation and upholding the principle of free speech is delicate and requires ongoing dialogue and consideration. Understanding defamation of character is crucial for anyone who engages in communication, whether in personal interactions or through public platforms, as the potential for harm is ever-present. It serves as a reminder of the power of words and the responsibility that accompanies them.

What Is An Allen Charge?

An Allen charge, often referred to as a "dynamite charge," is a specific instruction given by a judge to a deadlocked jury. This occurs when jurors find themselves unable to reach a unanimous decision after deliberating on a case. The term originates from a landmark case in the United States, Allen v. United States, which was decided by the Supreme Court in 1896. The essence of the Allen charge is to encourage jurors to re-examine their positions and consider the perspectives of their fellow jurors, with the hope of breaking the impasse and reaching a verdict.

The rationale behind the Allen charge is rooted in the judicial system's desire to avoid mistrials, which can be costly and time-consuming for all parties involved. When a jury cannot come to a consensus, it not only prolongs the legal process but also places an emotional burden on the individuals involved, from the defendants and the plaintiffs to the jurors themselves. Thus, the Allen charge serves as a tool to promote efficiency in the judicial system while also reinforcing the importance of collaboration and open-mindedness among jurors.

When a judge issues an Allen charge, it typically includes several key components. First, the judge will remind jurors of their duty to deliberate thoroughly and consider the evidence presented during the trial. This reminder emphasizes the importance of their role in the justice system and the weight of their collective responsibility. The judge may also encourage jurors to listen to one another, to engage in respectful dialogue about their differing viewpoints, and to be willing to reconsider their own positions in light of new arguments or perspectives.

It is important to note that while an Allen charge can be effective in prompting jurors to reach a verdict, it must be delivered carefully and judiciously. Overly forceful or coercive language can lead to concerns about the integrity of the jury's decision-making process. The goal is to foster a spirit of collaboration rather than to pressure jurors into conforming to a majority opinion. The balance is delicate; the judge must inspire jurors to continue deliberating without undermining their autonomy or the principle of a fair trial.

Critics of the Allen charge argue that it can create an undue influence on jurors, especially those who may be more susceptible to pressure from their peers. In some cases, this can lead to a verdict that does not accurately reflect the juror's true beliefs or understanding of the case. This concern has led to ongoing debates about the appropriateness of the Allen charge and its implications for the jury system as a whole. Some jurisdictions have even opted to modify or abandon the use of the Allen charge altogether, seeking alternative methods to address jury deadlock.

Despite these criticisms, the Allen charge remains a common practice in many courts across the United States. Its effectiveness often hinges on the specific context of the case and the dynamics of the jury involved. In some instances, a well-crafted Allen charge can successfully prompt jurors to re-engage with the evidence and arguments presented, leading to a resolution that reflects a thoughtful consideration of the case. In other situations, however, it may only serve to prolong deliberations or result in a verdict that is less than satisfactory to all parties involved.

Ultimately, the Allen charge represents a fascinating intersection of law, psychology, and human behavior. It highlights the complexities of group decision-making and the challenges inherent in achieving consensus among diverse perspectives. As jurors navigate the intricate landscape of their deliberations, the Allen charge serves as both a guiding light and a potential source of tension, embodying the delicate balance between judicial efficiency and the pursuit of justice. In the end, it is a reminder of the weighty responsibility that jurors carry as they strive to fulfill their duty to the court and to one another.

What Is Entrapment?

Entrapment is a legal defense that arises when an individual is induced or persuaded by law enforcement to commit a crime that they would not have otherwise committed. The concept of entrapment is rooted in the principle of fairness in the justice system, particularly the idea that the government should not create criminals through coercive or deceptive tactics. To understand entrapment fully, it's essential to delve into its historical context, legal definitions, and its implications in criminal cases.

Historically, the notion of entrapment can be traced back to the early 20th century, with significant legal cases shaping its interpretation. One of the most pivotal moments occurred in 1932 with the case of Sorrells v. United States, where the Supreme Court ruled that entrapment could serve as a valid defense if it could be shown that the government had instigated the crime. This case set a precedent, establishing that merely providing an opportunity to commit a crime does not constitute entrapment; rather, it is the method of persuasion that matters. If law enforcement officials use tactics that are excessively coercive or manipulative, it raises ethical questions about the integrity of the justice system.

Legally, entrapment is divided into two main tests: the subjective test and the objective test. The subjective test focuses on the defendant's predisposition to commit the crime. If an individual was already inclined to engage in criminal behavior, then they may not successfully argue entrapment, regardless of the methods used by law enforcement. Conversely, the objective test examines the conduct of law enforcement officers. If their actions are deemed overly aggressive or deceitful, the court may find that entrapment has occurred, regardless of the defendant's predisposition. This dual framework allows for a nuanced analysis of each case, recognizing that both the individual's intent and the state's conduct are critical factors.

The implications of entrapment in criminal cases are significant. When a defendant successfully proves entrapment, it can lead to the dismissal of charges or a not guilty verdict. This outcome serves not only to protect individuals from unethical law enforcement practices but also reinforces the principle that society should not condone the creation of criminals through manipulation. However, the entrapment defense is not without controversy. Critics argue that it can be misused by defendants seeking to evade responsibility for their actions. This concern highlights the delicate balance the legal system must maintain, ensuring that justice is served while protecting individual rights.

Moreover, entrapment raises broader questions about the role of law enforcement in society. The tactics employed by police in undercover operations or sting operations can blur the lines between lawful enforcement and coercion. For instance, in cases involving drug trafficking or prostitution, undercover officers may engage in behavior that some argue is overly persuasive, leading individuals to commit crimes they might not have otherwise considered. This dynamic can create a moral dilemma: at what point does law enforcement's duty to prevent crime cross into the territory of creating crime?

The discussion surrounding entrapment also intersects with issues of socioeconomic status and access to legal resources. Defendants from marginalized communities may face greater challenges in proving entrapment due to systemic inequalities within the legal system. This disparity raises questions about fairness and justice, as those with fewer resources may struggle to mount a successful defense against complex legal arguments.

In conclusion, entrapment is a multifaceted legal defense that embodies critical questions about justice, ethics, and the role of law enforcement. It serves as a reminder that while the pursuit of crime prevention is essential, the methods employed must adhere to principles of fairness and integrity. As society continues to grapple with these issues, understanding entrapment becomes crucial in fostering a justice system that respects individual rights while effectively addressing crime.

What Is A Soundproof Room?

A soundproof room, often referred to as an acoustically treated space, is designed specifically to prevent sound from entering or exiting its boundaries. The concept of soundproofing is rooted in the principles of acoustics, which is the science of sound and its behavior in different environments. Essentially, soundproofing aims to create an environment where sound waves are effectively absorbed, blocked, or diffused, ensuring that the sounds generated within the room remain contained and that external noises are kept at bay.

To understand what makes a room soundproof, we must first consider the nature of sound itself. Sound is a mechanical wave that travels through air, water, or solid materials, and it can be characterized by its frequency and amplitude. High-frequency sounds, like a whistle or a scream, tend to be more easily absorbed by soft materials, while low-frequency sounds, such as bass from music or machinery, can penetrate through walls and other barriers more easily. This distinction is crucial when designing a soundproof room, as it informs the choice of materials and construction techniques used.

One of the primary methods of soundproofing involves adding mass to the walls, ceilings, and floors of a room. Heavier materials, such as concrete or specialized soundproof drywall, can significantly reduce sound transmission. The principle here is straightforward: the more massive a barrier is, the harder it is for sound waves to pass through. Additionally, soundproofing techniques often involve creating air gaps or using resilient channels that decouple walls, allowing sound waves to dissipate before they reach the opposite side. This decoupling technique is particularly effective in minimizing sound transmission between rooms in a shared building.

Another critical aspect of soundproofing is the use of sound-absorbing materials. These materials are designed to minimize sound reflections within the room, thereby reducing echo and reverberation. Common sound-absorbing materials include acoustic panels, carpets, curtains, and specialized foam products that can be strategically placed on walls and ceilings. By absorbing sound waves, these materials help to create a quieter, more controlled auditory environment. In practice, a well-soundproofed room will not only keep outside noise from intruding but will also improve the quality of sound within the space, making it ideal for activities such as music recording, film editing, or even meditation.

Ventilation is another important consideration in soundproof room design. A completely sealed room can lead to air quality issues, so it's essential to incorporate soundproof ventilation systems that allow for airflow without compromising sound isolation. This is often achieved through the use of specially designed ducts and silencers that minimize the transmission of sound while still providing adequate ventilation. Through careful planning and engineering, a soundproof room can maintain a comfortable atmosphere while effectively isolating sound.

The applications of soundproof rooms are vast and varied. They are commonly found in recording studios, rehearsal spaces, home theaters, and even offices where confidentiality is paramount. In residential settings, soundproofing can enhance privacy, allowing individuals to enjoy their activities without disturbing others. In commercial environments, soundproofing can improve productivity by reducing distractions from outside noise.

Ultimately, a soundproof room is not just about silence; it's about creating a controlled auditory environment that enhances the experience of sound itself. Whether for artistic expression, professional work, or personal enjoyment, the principles of soundproofing can transform a space into a sanctuary for sound. Understanding the science behind soundproofing opens up new possibilities for how we engage with the auditory world around us, allowing us to craft environments that cater to our specific needs and preferences. In a world filled with noise, the importance of soundproofing cannot be overstated; it offers a refuge, a place where sound can be both contained and celebrated.

What Are Cinder Blocks?

Cinder blocks, also known as concrete masonry units, are essential building materials that have been used for decades in construction. They are made from a mixture of cement, water, and aggregates, which can include sand, gravel, or crushed stone. The result is a lightweight, durable block that is easy to handle and provides excellent structural integrity. Typically, a standard cinder block measures 16 inches long, 8 inches high, and 8 inches deep, although variations exist to suit different construction needs.

One of the primary advantages of cinder blocks is their thermal mass. This means they can absorb and store heat, helping to regulate indoor temperatures. In regions with fluctuating climates, this property can lead to significant energy savings, as buildings constructed with cinder blocks can stay cooler in the summer and warmer in the winter. Additionally, cinder blocks are fire-resistant, making them a popular choice for building walls that need to withstand extreme heat.

Cinder blocks are also highly versatile. They can be used for various applications, including foundations, walls, and even decorative features. Their hollow cores can be filled with concrete or insulation, enhancing their strength and energy efficiency. The blocks can be easily cut or shaped, allowing for creative architectural designs.

Moreover, cinder blocks are eco-friendly. They can be produced using recycled materials, reducing waste and the carbon footprint associated with traditional building materials. Their longevity and low maintenance requirements further contribute to their sustainability.

In summary, cinder blocks are a practical and versatile choice in the construction industry. Their unique properties, including thermal mass, fire resistance, and eco-friendliness, make them an invaluable resource for builders and architects alike. Understanding what cinder blocks are and their benefits can help anyone appreciate their role in modern construction.

What Is Bakelite?

Bakelite, often hailed as the first synthetic plastic, stands as a remarkable testament to human ingenuity and innovation. Developed in the early 20th century by Belgian chemist Leo Baekeland, this material emerged from a quest to create a durable, heat-resistant substance that could replace natural materials like ivory and tortoiseshell. The year was 1907 when Baekeland first synthesized Bakelite, transforming a mixture of phenol and formaldehyde under heat and pressure. This groundbreaking invention marked the dawn of the plastic age, forever altering manufacturing and consumer culture.

What sets Bakelite apart from other materials is its unique chemical structure. Unlike thermoplastics, which can be melted and reshaped, Bakelite is a thermosetting plastic. This means that once it is molded and set, it cannot be remelted or reshaped. The polymerization process that creates Bakelite involves a cross-linking of molecules, resulting in a rigid, inflexible structure that boasts exceptional strength and durability. This characteristic made Bakelite an ideal candidate for a wide range of applications, from electrical insulators to household items.

The versatility of Bakelite is one of its most significant attributes. In the early 20th century, it found its way into various industries, playing a crucial role in the production of electrical components. Bakelite's excellent insulating properties made it a preferred choice for switches, sockets, and circuit boards, ensuring safety and reliability in electrical devices. Beyond the realm of electronics, Bakelite also made a splash in the world of fashion and design. Its ability to be molded into intricate shapes allowed for the creation of stylish jewelry, buttons, and decorative objects. The vibrant colors and glossy finishes of Bakelite pieces quickly captivated consumers, leading to a surge in popularity during the 1920s and 1930s.

However, Bakelite's impact was not limited to aesthetics and functionality. It also played a significant role in the development of modern manufacturing techniques. The ability to mass-produce Bakelite products led to the rise of consumer culture, as items that were once handcrafted became accessible to the general public at a fraction of the cost. This democratization of design and production paved the way for a new era of consumerism, where people could purchase affordable, stylish goods for their homes and personal use.

As the years progressed, Bakelite found its place in various sectors, including automotive and furniture industries. Car manufacturers embraced Bakelite for its lightweight and durable qualities, using it for dashboard components, knobs, and trim. In the realm of furniture, designers utilized Bakelite to create modern, streamlined pieces that reflected the aesthetics of the mid-century design movement. The material became synonymous with modernity, embodying the spirit of innovation that characterized the 20th century.

Despite its many advantages, Bakelite is not without its drawbacks. The production process involves the use of formaldehyde, a substance that can be harmful to human health and the environment. As awareness of these issues grew, the popularity of Bakelite began to wane, giving way to newer, safer alternatives. Today, while Bakelite may not dominate the market as it once did, it remains a beloved material among collectors and enthusiasts. Vintage Bakelite jewelry and household items are highly sought after, celebrated for their craftsmanship and historical significance.

In conclusion, Bakelite is more than just a plastic; it is a symbol of innovation, a reflection of cultural shifts, and a bridge between the natural and synthetic worlds. Its legacy endures, reminding us of a time when creativity and technology converged to create something truly revolutionary. As we navigate the complexities of modern materials and sustainability, Bakelite serves as a reminder of the delicate balance between progress and responsibility, urging us to consider the impact of our inventions on both society and the planet.

What Is Fiberglass?

Fiberglass, a term that might evoke images of boats gliding across shimmering waters or the sleek contours of modern buildings, is a composite material that has revolutionized various industries since its inception. But what exactly is fiberglass? At its core, fiberglass is a type of reinforced plastic made from a matrix of glass fibers embedded in a resin. This combination yields a material that possesses remarkable strength, durability, and resistance to corrosion, making it a popular choice in construction, automotive, aerospace, and even household applications.

To understand fiberglass, we must first delve into its components. The glass fibers, which are the backbone of this material, are typically made from silica, a compound abundant in sand. These fibers are drawn into thin strands that can be woven together or left as loose filaments. The process of creating glass fibers involves melting raw materials at extremely high temperatures, around 1,700 degrees Celsius, and then rapidly cooling them to form solid strands. The result is a lightweight yet incredibly strong material that can be manipulated in various ways.

The resin used in fiberglass is usually a thermosetting polymer, most commonly epoxy, polyester, or vinyl ester. This resin acts as a binding agent, holding the glass fibers together and providing the material with its unique properties. When the resin is mixed with a hardener and applied to the glass fibers, it undergoes a chemical reaction that causes it to harden. This process not only solidifies the structure but also enhances the strength and durability of the fiberglass, allowing it to withstand considerable stress and strain.

One of the most significant advantages of fiberglass is its versatility. It can be molded into virtually any shape, allowing for a wide range of applications. In the marine industry, fiberglass is favored for boat hulls due to its lightweight nature and resistance to water damage. Unlike traditional materials like wood or metal, fiberglass does not rot or corrode, ensuring longevity and reducing maintenance costs. Similarly, in the automotive sector, fiberglass is used for body panels, ensuring vehicles are both lightweight and fuel-efficient while maintaining structural integrity.

In construction, fiberglass has found its way into insulation materials, roofing, and even reinforced concrete. Fiberglass insulation, for example, is known for its excellent thermal properties, helping to keep homes warm in winter and cool in summer. Moreover, its non-combustible nature makes it a safe choice for building materials, providing an added layer of security against fire hazards.

However, it is essential to acknowledge that fiberglass is not without its challenges. The production process can be energy-intensive, and the disposal of fiberglass products can pose environmental concerns. Unlike organic materials, fiberglass does not decompose, leading to potential waste issues. Recycling fiberglass is possible, but it is not as straightforward as recycling metals or plastics, which can complicate efforts to minimize environmental impact.

Despite these challenges, fiberglass continues to evolve. Advances in technology have led to the development of more sustainable practices, including the use of recycled glass fibers and bio-based resins. Researchers are exploring innovative ways to enhance the recyclability of fiberglass, aiming to reduce its ecological footprint while maintaining the performance that has made it so popular.

In summary, fiberglass is a remarkable material that has transformed industries through its unique combination of strength, lightweight properties, and resistance to environmental factors. Its versatility allows it to be molded into various shapes, making it indispensable in applications ranging from marine vessels to construction materials. As we continue to innovate and address the environmental challenges associated with its production and disposal, fiberglass stands as a testament to human ingenuity and the ongoing quest for better, more sustainable materials. Whether it's a sleek boat slicing through waves or insulation keeping a home cozy, fiberglass is quietly shaping the world around us, a silent yet powerful force in modern manufacturing and design.

What Are Ball Bearings?

Ball bearings are fascinating little devices that play a crucial role in the machinery and technology we encounter every day. At their core, ball bearings are used to reduce friction between moving parts. Imagine a world without them; machinery would be less efficient, wear out faster, and operate at higher temperatures. The basic design of a ball bearing consists of a series of small steel balls housed between two smooth surfaces, known as races. These balls allow for smooth, rolling motion, which minimizes the friction that would occur if two surfaces were simply sliding against each other.

The principle behind ball bearings is relatively simple, yet incredibly effective. When a load is applied, the balls distribute that load evenly across the surface of the races. This distribution decreases the surface area in contact, thereby reducing friction and wear. You can find ball bearings in countless applications, from the wheels of a skateboard to the intricate workings of a jet engine.

The history of ball bearings dates back to ancient times. The earliest known use was in the 4th century BC when the Roman architect Vitruvius described a method for using wooden balls to reduce friction in a device. However, it wasn't until the 19th century that modern ball bearings were developed, significantly improving efficiency in machinery during the Industrial Revolution.

Different types of ball bearings exist, including deep groove, angular contact, and thrust bearings, each designed for specific applications and load conditions. The material of the balls can vary as well, with options like stainless steel, ceramic, or plastic, depending on the environment and required durability. In essence, ball bearings are unsung heroes of modern engineering, ensuring that our machines run smoothly and efficiently, making our lives easier and more productive.

What Is A Bulldozer?

A bulldozer, at first glance, might appear to be just another piece of heavy machinery, a mere tool in the vast arsenal of construction equipment. However, to truly understand what a bulldozer is, one must delve deeper into its purpose, design, and the pivotal role it plays in various industries. A bulldozer is a powerful, tracked vehicle equipped with a broad, flat blade at the front, designed primarily for pushing large quantities of soil, sand, rubble, or other materials during construction or excavation projects. Its tracks provide superior traction and stability, enabling it to traverse uneven terrain that would challenge wheeled vehicles.

The origins of the bulldozer can be traced back to the early 20th century, evolving from the simpler steam-powered tractors that were used for agricultural purposes. As industrialization progressed, the need for more robust machinery became evident, leading to the development of the modern bulldozer. The first true bulldozer was introduced in the 1920s, featuring a blade that could be raised and lowered, allowing for greater versatility in its operations. Over the decades, advancements in technology have transformed bulldozers into sophisticated machines equipped with hydraulic systems, GPS, and even automated controls, enhancing their efficiency and ease of use.

One of the most remarkable aspects of a bulldozer is its versatility. While primarily associated with construction, bulldozers are utilized in a variety of applications. They play a crucial role in road construction, where they clear paths, level surfaces, and move debris. In mining, bulldozers are instrumental in the removal of overburden, allowing access to valuable minerals beneath the earth's surface. In agriculture, they assist in land clearing and preparation, making way for crops to grow. Even in disaster response, bulldozers are employed to clear debris after natural disasters, facilitating rescue operations and the rebuilding process.

The bulldozer's blade is perhaps its most defining feature, available in various shapes and sizes depending on the intended application. The straight blade, or S-blade, is ideal for pushing and leveling materials, while the universal blade, or U-blade, is designed for carrying and digging. There are also angle blades that can be adjusted to push materials to the side, allowing for more precise control in tight spaces. This adaptability makes the bulldozer an indispensable tool in many industries.

In addition to its physical attributes, the bulldozer is powered by a robust engine typically ranging from 50 to over 1,000 horsepower, depending on the size and intended use of the machine. This power enables the bulldozer to perform demanding tasks, such as pushing heavy loads or scraping surfaces, with relative ease. The operator's skill is also a crucial factor; a well-trained operator can maximize the bulldozer's capabilities, maneuvering it with precision to achieve the desired results.

Safety is paramount when operating a bulldozer, given its size and weight. Operators must be aware of their surroundings and adhere to safety protocols to prevent accidents. Modern bulldozers often come equipped with safety features such as roll-over protective structures (ROPS) and seat belts, designed to protect the operator in the event of a mishap.

As urbanization continues to expand and infrastructure projects become increasingly complex, the demand for bulldozers remains strong. They are not just machines; they are the backbone of construction, shaping the world we live in. From clearing land for new buildings to creating roads that connect communities, bulldozers are essential in transforming landscapes and facilitating progress. In a world that constantly evolves, the bulldozer stands as a testament to human ingenuity, a powerful ally in the quest to build and expand, pushing boundaries and reshaping our environment, one load at a time. Understanding what a bulldozer is reveals the intricate relationship between technology and construction, a relationship that continues to evolve with each passing day.

How Do Elevators Work?

Elevators, those ubiquitous metal boxes that whisk us up and down in buildings, are marvels of engineering, combining physics, mechanics, and technology to transport us safely between floors. At their core, elevators operate on a simple principle: they use a system of pulleys, cables, and counterweights to move the cab vertically. But let's dive deeper into how this intricate system works, starting from the basic components.

First, we have the elevator cab itself, which is the part that carries passengers or freight. This cab is suspended by a set of steel cables, typically made from high-strength steel to ensure durability and safety. These cables are attached to a pulley system located at the top of the elevator shaft. When the elevator is called to a floor, an electric motor activates, turning the pulley and either raising or lowering the cab. This is where the counterweight comes into play. The counterweight is a heavy block that balances the weight of the cab, making it easier for the motor to move the cab. When the elevator cab goes up, the counterweight goes down, and vice versa. This system reduces the amount of energy needed to lift the cab, making the operation more efficient.

Now, let's talk about the control system, which is the brain behind the operation of the elevator. When you press a button to call the elevator, a signal is sent to the control panel, which processes the request and determines the most efficient way to respond. The control panel manages the motor, ensuring that it operates at the right speed and direction. Modern elevators often use advanced algorithms to optimize travel routes, reducing wait times and improving efficiency, especially in high-rise buildings where multiple elevators might be in operation at the same time.

Safety is paramount in elevator design. Elevators are equipped with a variety of safety features to protect passengers. One of the most critical is the brake system. If the cables were to snap, the brakes would engage automatically, preventing the cab from falling. Additionally, there are safety buffers at the bottom of the elevator shaft that can absorb the impact in case of a malfunction. Regular maintenance checks are essential to ensure all components are functioning correctly, and most elevators are designed to undergo routine inspections to uphold safety standards.

Another important aspect of elevators is the type of system they use. The most common type is the traction elevator, which utilizes the pulley and counterweight system we've discussed. However, there are also hydraulic elevators that operate differently. Instead of cables and pulleys, hydraulic elevators use a fluid-driven piston to raise and lower the cab. This type is often found in low-rise buildings due to its limitations in height and speed. In contrast, pneumatic elevators use air pressure to move the cab, offering a unique and modern design that can be an aesthetic feature in residential settings.

As buildings continue to rise higher and higher, the technology behind elevators must also evolve. Engineers are now exploring the use of magnetic levitation, similar to high-speed trains, which could allow elevators to move both vertically and horizontally, revolutionizing how we think about vertical transportation in skyscrapers. This innovation could lead to the development of multi-directional elevators that can travel across multiple shafts, drastically reducing wait times and improving efficiency.

In conclusion, elevators are a fascinating blend of physics, engineering, and technology. From the basic mechanics of pulleys and counterweights to advanced control systems and safety features, every part of an elevator is designed to ensure a smooth and safe ride. As we continue to build taller and smarter buildings, the evolution of elevator technology will play a crucial role in shaping the future of urban architecture and transportation. So the next time you step into an elevator, take a moment to appreciate the intricate system that makes your journey possible, a hidden marvel operating just above your head, silently working to lift you to new heights.

What Is Smell-O-Vision?

Imagine a world where the cinema experience transcends the visual and auditory realms, where the scent of fresh popcorn wafts through the air, mingling with the aroma of rain-soaked earth or the sweet fragrance of blooming flowers, all while you're seated in a darkened theater. This is the essence of Smell-O-Vision, a concept that has long fascinated filmmakers, marketers, and audiences alike. But what exactly is Smell-O-Vision? At its core, Smell-O-Vision is a technology designed to enhance the movie-watching experience by integrating olfactory stimuli into film presentations, allowing viewers to not only see and hear the story but also to smell it.

The origins of Smell-O-Vision date back to the mid-20th century, a time when the film industry was searching for innovative ways to attract audiences away from their television sets and back into theaters. The first notable attempt to bring smell to the cinema was in 1959, when a film called "Scent of Mystery" was released. This movie was equipped with a system that released specific scents at key moments in the film, allowing viewers to experience the story on a whole new sensory level. Imagine a scene where a character strolls through a fragrant garden; as they inhale the sweet scent of roses, the audience would also be enveloped in that same aroma. The idea was revolutionary, but the execution was less than perfect. Many viewers found the scents distracting or poorly timed, leading to mixed reviews and ultimately, the demise of the technology in mainstream cinema.

Despite its rocky beginnings, the concept of Smell-O-Vision has persisted, evolving over the decades. The idea of incorporating smell into entertainment is not limited to film; it has found its way into theme parks, virtual reality experiences, and even video games. The technology has advanced, with modern systems utilizing scent dispensers that can release a variety of fragrances in precise synchronization with visual and auditory cues. This means filmmakers can craft a more immersive experience, pulling audiences deeper into their narratives. Imagine watching a thrilling chase scene as the scent of burning rubber fills the air, or a romantic moment accompanied by the delicate perfume of blooming jasmine. The possibilities are tantalizing.

However, the implementation of Smell-O-Vision is not without its challenges. One major hurdle is the complexity of scent delivery systems. Creating a wide range of scents that are both pleasant and accurately timed with the film's action requires a level of precision that is difficult to achieve. Additionally, the logistics of maintaining scent dispensers in theaters, ensuring they are clean and functioning properly, poses another layer of difficulty. There's also the question of audience preferences; not everyone enjoys the same scents, and what is delightful to one person may be off-putting to another. The challenge lies in striking a balance between enhancing the experience and overwhelming the senses.

Moreover, there are cultural considerations to take into account. Scents can evoke powerful memories and emotions, but these associations are deeply personal and can vary widely across different cultures. A scent that is comforting to one person may be entirely foreign or even unpleasant to another. This variability complicates the task of creating a universally appealing olfactory experience in a shared space like a movie theater.

Despite these challenges, the allure of Smell-O-Vision remains strong. It taps into a fundamental aspect of human experience: our sense of smell is intricately linked to memory and emotion. By engaging this sense, filmmakers have the potential to create a richer narrative tapestry, one that resonates on a deeper level with viewers. As technology continues to advance, the dream of a fully immersive cinematic experience, where sight, sound, and smell converge, may not be as far-fetched as it once seemed. Smell-O-Vision, while still in its infancy, represents a fascinating intersection of art and science, inviting us to imagine a future where the stories we love come to life in ways we've only begun to explore.

What Is A Weeder Class?

A weeder class is essentially a course designed to help students determine whether they are truly suited for a particular academic path or major. The term often refers to introductory courses in challenging fields, like pre-med or engineering, where the material is intentionally rigorous. The idea is to "weed out" those who may not have the aptitude or passion for the subject matter. These classes serve a dual purpose: they provide essential foundational knowledge while also acting as a litmus test for students' commitment to their chosen discipline.

In many universities, weeder classes are notorious for their difficulty. They often have high dropout rates, as students quickly realize that the demands of the course exceed their expectations. This can be disheartening, but it's crucial for students to understand that these classes are not merely obstacles; they are opportunities for self-discovery. By facing challenging material, students can assess their strengths and weaknesses, allowing them to make informed decisions about their academic futures.

Moreover, weeder classes can foster resilience. They push students to develop effective study habits and time management skills, essential tools for success in any field. While the experience may be daunting, those who persevere often emerge with a stronger grasp of the subject and a clearer understanding of their academic goals.

However, the concept of weeder classes is not without controversy. Critics argue that they can disproportionately affect students from less privileged backgrounds, who may not have access to the same preparatory resources as their peers. This raises important questions about equity in education. Ultimately, a weeder class is more than just a hurdle; it's a pivotal moment in a student's journey, shaping not only their academic trajectory but also their personal growth.

Why Are Broken Legs Dangerous For Horses?

When we think about horses, we often envision their strength, grace, and agility. They are magnificent creatures, built for speed and endurance, yet beneath that powerful exterior lies a vulnerability that can lead to dire consequences—especially when it comes to injuries like broken legs. Understanding why broken legs are dangerous for horses requires us to delve into their anatomy, the nature of their injuries, and the implications for their health and well-being.

First, let's consider the anatomy of a horse. Horses are large animals, and their legs are designed to support their weight while allowing for incredible movement. Unlike humans, horses have evolved with a unique skeletal structure that includes long, slender bones, and a complex system of tendons and ligaments. This design is efficient for running and jumping but also makes their legs particularly susceptible to fractures. A broken leg in a horse is not just a simple injury; it can be a catastrophic event that threatens the horse's life.

When a horse sustains a broken leg, the type of fracture plays a crucial role in determining the outcome. There are several types of fractures, ranging from hairline cracks to complete breaks that shatter the bone. The severity of the fracture often dictates the treatment options available. Some fractures can be repaired with surgery, involving the insertion of pins or plates to stabilize the bone. However, even with surgical intervention, there are no guarantees. Horses have a high risk of complications, including infection, poor healing, or even the development of laminitis, a painful condition affecting the hooves that can arise from the stress of injury.

Moreover, the sheer size and weight of a horse compound the dangers associated with broken legs. When a horse breaks a leg, the animal instinctively tries to shift its weight away from the injured limb, leading to uneven distribution of weight across the other legs. This can result in further injuries or even fractures in the uninjured legs. The situation becomes a vicious cycle, as the horse struggles to maintain balance and mobility while dealing with pain and the limitations imposed by the injury.

Another critical aspect to consider is the psychological impact of a broken leg on a horse. Horses are prey animals, and their instinct is to flee from danger. When faced with an injury that limits their ability to move, the psychological stress can be immense. They may exhibit signs of anxiety, fear, or depression, which can hinder their recovery. The bond between horse and rider or caretaker becomes vital in these situations, as a calm and supportive environment can make a significant difference in the horse's mental state.

Furthermore, the economic implications of a broken leg cannot be overlooked. For many horse owners, a horse is not just a pet; it is an investment. The costs associated with veterinary care, surgery, rehabilitation, and potential long-term care can be staggering. In some cases, the financial burden may lead owners to make difficult decisions about the horse's future, including the heartbreaking choice of euthanasia if the injury is deemed irreparable. This reality underscores the importance of preventive measures, such as proper training, safe environments, and regular veterinary care.

In conclusion, broken legs are dangerous for horses due to a combination of anatomical vulnerabilities, the nature of the injuries, psychological impacts, and economic considerations. The consequences of such an injury can be life-altering, not just for the horse but also for its owner. Understanding these factors highlights the need for responsible horse ownership and the importance of safeguarding these majestic animals from the risks that can lead to such devastating injuries. The fragility of a horse's leg serves as a poignant reminder of the delicate balance between strength and vulnerability in the animal kingdom.

How Does A Superconductor Work?

Superconductors are fascinating materials that exhibit a remarkable property: they can conduct electricity without any resistance when cooled below a certain critical temperature. This phenomenon is not only intriguing but also has profound implications for technology and energy efficiency. To understand how superconductors work, we need to delve into the underlying principles of superconductivity, which was first discovered in 1911 by Dutch physicist Heike Kamerlingh Onnes when he observed that mercury, when cooled to a temperature near absolute zero, lost all electrical resistance.

At the heart of superconductivity lies the concept of electron pairing. In normal conductive materials, such as copper or aluminum, electrons move through a lattice of atoms. As they do so, they encounter resistance due to collisions with impurities and lattice vibrations, known as phonons. This resistance generates heat and energy loss, which is why electrical wires get warm when current flows through them. However, in superconductors, something extraordinary happens. Below the critical temperature, electrons form pairs known as Cooper pairs. This pairing is not a simple attraction; it arises from a delicate balance between the attractive forces mediated by phonons and the repulsive forces between electrons due to their negative charge.

These Cooper pairs behave quite differently from individual electrons. Instead of scattering and colliding with the lattice, they move through the material in a coordinated manner, much like a flock of birds flying in formation. This collective behavior allows them to glide through the lattice without resistance. The formation of Cooper pairs is a quantum mechanical phenomenon, and it is this quantum nature that sets superconductors apart from ordinary conductors. The pairs condense into a collective ground state, and it is this state that allows for the zero-resistance property.

Now, you might wonder why all materials don't become superconductors at room temperature. The answer lies in the specific conditions required for Cooper pair formation. Each material has a unique critical temperature, determined by its atomic structure and the interactions between its electrons and lattice. Some materials, like elemental lead or niobium, become superconductors at relatively low temperatures, while others, known as high-temperature superconductors, can operate at temperatures above the boiling point of liquid nitrogen, around 77 Kelvin. These high-temperature superconductors are often ceramic compounds, and their mechanism of superconductivity is still an area of active research.

Another important aspect of superconductors is the Meissner effect, which describes their ability to expel magnetic fields. When a material transitions into the superconducting state, it will repel magnetic field lines, causing a magnet to levitate above it. This effect is not just a curious phenomenon; it has practical applications in magnetic levitation technologies, such as maglev trains, which can travel at incredible speeds with minimal friction.

Superconductors have a wide range of applications, from medical imaging technologies like MRI machines to particle accelerators and quantum computers. In the realm of energy, they hold the potential to revolutionize power grids by enabling lossless transmission of electricity over long distances. Imagine a world where energy is transmitted without loss, where electric vehicles charge in minutes, and where magnetic levitation allows for ultra-fast transportation. The possibilities are vast, but there are challenges to overcome, particularly in maintaining the extreme cooling required for many superconductors.

As research continues, scientists are exploring new materials and methods to achieve superconductivity at higher temperatures, seeking to unlock the full potential of this extraordinary phenomenon. The quest for room-temperature superconductors is one of the holy grails of modern physics, and achieving this breakthrough could lead to a new era of technological advancements. In conclusion, superconductors work through the unique pairing of electrons into Cooper pairs, allowing them to move without resistance and expel magnetic fields, and their potential applications could reshape our technological landscape for generations to come.

What Is A Mobius Strip?

Imagine a piece of paper, a simple strip, like the kind you might find in a notebook. Now, take that strip and give it a twist, just a single, half twist, and then join the ends together. What you've created is a Möbius strip, a fascinating object that defies our conventional understanding of surfaces and dimensions. The Möbius strip is not just a curious shape; it's a profound mathematical concept that challenges our perceptions of geometry and topology. It's named after August Ferdinand Möbius, a German mathematician who, along with Johann Benedict Listing, discovered this intriguing surface in the 19th century.

At first glance, the Möbius strip appears to be a simple loop, but it possesses a unique property that sets it apart from ordinary loops. If you were to take a pencil and start drawing a line down the center of the strip, you would find that you can continue drawing without ever lifting your pencil off the surface. You would eventually return to your starting point, having drawn a continuous line that covers both sides of the strip. This single-sided nature is what makes the Möbius strip so captivating; it has only one surface and one edge. In a world where we are accustomed to thinking in terms of two-sided objects, the Möbius strip invites us to reconsider the very essence of surfaces.

The implications of this simple twist extend far beyond mere curiosity. The Möbius strip has found its way into various fields of study, including mathematics, art, and even science. In topology, which is the study of properties that remain unchanged under continuous deformations, the Möbius strip serves as a prime example of a non-orientable surface. This means that if you were to navigate around the strip, you could find yourself on what appears to be the "opposite" side without ever crossing an edge. It challenges our intuitive understanding of left and right, inside and outside, and emphasizes the complexity of spatial relationships.

Artists and designers have also been inspired by the Möbius strip. Its elegant form has been used in sculptures, jewelry, and architecture, symbolizing infinity and the interconnectedness of all things. It serves as a metaphor for unity and continuity, suggesting that opposing forces can coexist harmoniously. The strip has even appeared in literature and popular culture, representing the idea that life is a continuous journey with no clear beginning or end.

In the realm of science, the Möbius strip has practical applications as well. It has been explored in the context of materials science, where researchers have studied its unique properties to develop stronger and more flexible materials. The concept has also been applied in the field of robotics and engineering, where it can be used to create efficient designs and mechanisms that optimize space and resources.

Moreover, the Möbius strip offers a fascinating perspective on mathematics itself. It serves as an entry point into the broader world of mathematical concepts, encouraging exploration and curiosity. It reminds us that mathematics is not just a collection of numbers and equations but a language that describes the world around us. The beauty of the Möbius strip lies in its ability to bridge the gap between abstract mathematical theory and tangible, real-world applications.

In conclusion, the Möbius strip is more than just a simple geometric figure; it is a symbol of the unexpected and the extraordinary. It invites us to look closer, to question our assumptions, and to embrace the complexity of the world we inhabit. Whether we encounter it in mathematics, art, or science, the Möbius strip serves as a reminder that there is always more than meets the eye, and that the simplest ideas can lead to the most profound insights. It challenges us to think differently, to explore the infinite possibilities that lie within a single twist.

What Is Schrodinger's Cat?

Schrödinger's Cat is a thought experiment devised by the Austrian physicist Erwin Schrödinger in 1935, designed to illustrate the peculiarities of quantum mechanics and the concept of superposition. At its core, the thought experiment presents a scenario that challenges our classical intuitions about reality, particularly regarding measurement and observation. Imagine a cat placed inside a sealed box alongside a radioactive atom, a Geiger counter, a vial of poison, and a hammer. The setup is such that if the radioactive atom decays, the Geiger counter triggers the hammer, which then breaks the vial of poison, leading to the cat's demise. Conversely, if the atom does not decay, the cat remains alive.

Now, here's where it gets interesting. Quantum mechanics tells us that until we open the box and observe the system, the atom exists in a superposition of states—both decayed and not decayed simultaneously. Consequently, the cat, too, is in a superposition: it is both alive and dead at the same time. This paradox highlights the strangeness of quantum mechanics, where particles can exist in multiple states until an observation is made.

The thought experiment raises profound questions about the nature of reality and the role of the observer. In classical physics, objects have definite states, independent of observation. However, in the quantum realm, the act of measuring or observing a system seems to influence its state. This leads to the philosophical dilemma of what it means for something to exist in a particular state. Is reality dependent on our observation, or does it exist independently of our perceptions?

Schrödinger's Cat also serves to illustrate the concept of wave function collapse. In quantum mechanics, particles are described by a wave function that encapsulates all possible states. When an observation occurs, this wave function collapses into a single state, which we then perceive as reality. In the case of the cat, when we open the box, we force the wave function to collapse; we either find the cat alive or dead, but not both. This collapse raises further questions about the nature of reality: does the wave function represent a real physical state, or is it merely a mathematical tool for predicting probabilities?

The implications of Schrödinger's Cat extend beyond theoretical physics. They touch upon the philosophical realms of determinism and free will. If the universe operates under the principles of quantum mechanics, where outcomes are probabilistic rather than deterministic, what does that mean for our understanding of choice and causality? Are our actions predetermined by the laws of physics, or do we possess the agency to influence outcomes?

Moreover, Schrödinger's Cat has become a cultural touchstone, referenced in discussions about consciousness, reality, and the nature of existence. It has inspired countless interpretations, from the purely scientific to the deeply philosophical, as thinkers grapple with its implications. Some argue that the thought experiment underscores the absurdity of applying quantum mechanics to everyday objects, while others see it as a compelling argument for the interconnectedness of observation and reality.

In contemporary physics, interpretations of quantum mechanics abound, from the Copenhagen interpretation, which emphasizes the role of the observer, to the many-worlds interpretation, which posits that all possible outcomes exist in parallel universes. Each interpretation attempts to reconcile the strange behavior of quantum particles with our macroscopic experience of reality, yet none has achieved universal acceptance.

Ultimately, Schrödinger's Cat serves as a powerful reminder of the limitations of our understanding. It illustrates that the universe operates in ways that often defy our intuitive grasp, inviting us to question our assumptions about existence, observation, and the very fabric of reality itself. In a world where a cat can be both alive and dead, we are left to ponder the nature of truth and the mysteries that lie at the intersection of science and philosophy.

What Is A Faraday Cage?

A Faraday cage is a fascinating and practical concept rooted in the principles of electromagnetism. Named after the English scientist Michael Faraday, who first demonstrated its effects in the 19th century, a Faraday cage is essentially an enclosure made of conductive materials that can block external static and non-static electric fields. The fundamental principle behind its operation lies in the way electric charges behave. When an external electric field encounters a conductive material, it induces charges within that material to rearrange themselves. This movement of charges creates an opposing electric field that cancels out the original field within the enclosure. As a result, the interior of a Faraday cage is shielded from external electromagnetic interference, making it a valuable tool in various applications.

One of the most common examples of a Faraday cage is the metal mesh or solid metal structure used in microwave ovens. The design of the oven ensures that the microwaves generated inside remain contained, preventing them from escaping and causing harm. Similarly, the metal body of a car acts as a Faraday cage during a lightning storm. When lightning strikes, the electrical charge travels along the surface of the car, protecting the occupants inside from the dangerous effects of the lightning. This phenomenon is critical to understand, especially in areas prone to thunderstorms, as it highlights the importance of seeking shelter in a vehicle rather than under a tree.

Faraday cages are not limited to everyday objects; they also play a significant role in scientific research and technology. In laboratories,

Faraday cages are used to create controlled environments for sensitive experiments. For instance, when researchers are studying the behavior of subatomic particles or conducting experiments involving electromagnetic radiation, they need to eliminate any external interference. By placing their equipment inside a Faraday cage, they can ensure that their measurements are accurate and reliable, free from the noise that external electromagnetic fields might introduce.

Moreover, Faraday cages are essential in the field of telecommunications. They are used to protect sensitive electronic equipment from electromagnetic interference, which can disrupt signals and lead to data loss. In data centers and server rooms, Faraday cages help maintain the integrity of the systems by shielding them from external sources of electromagnetic radiation. This is particularly crucial as our reliance on technology continues to grow, and the need for robust and secure communication systems becomes more pressing.

The design of a Faraday cage can vary significantly depending on its intended use. It can be as simple as a wire mesh structure or as complex as a room lined with conductive materials. The effectiveness of a Faraday cage depends on several factors, including the frequency of the electromagnetic waves it is meant to block and the size of the openings in the conductive material. Generally, the smaller the openings, the more effective the cage will be at blocking higher frequency waves. This principle is why certain types of shielding are necessary for different applications, from protecting sensitive electronics to ensuring the safety of individuals during electrical storms.

In addition to its practical applications, the concept of the Faraday cage has also sparked interest in popular culture. Movies and television shows often depict characters using makeshift Faraday cages to protect themselves from invasive technologies or electromagnetic attacks. While these portrayals may exaggerate the concept, they highlight a growing awareness of the importance of electromagnetic safety in our increasingly connected world.

In conclusion, a Faraday cage is a remarkable invention that serves a critical purpose in both everyday life and advanced scientific research. By understanding the principles behind its operation, we can appreciate its significance in protecting us from unwanted electromagnetic interference and ensuring the reliability of our technological systems. As we continue to navigate a world filled with electromagnetic signals, the Faraday cage remains a vital tool in safeguarding our devices and ourselves from the invisible forces that surround us.

What Is Amperage?

Amperage, often referred to simply as "amps," is a fundamental concept in the field of electricity and electronics. To understand amperage, we must first grasp the broader framework of electrical concepts, particularly the relationship between voltage, current, and resistance, which are encapsulated in Ohm's Law. This law states that the current flowing through a conductor between two points is directly proportional to the voltage across the two points and inversely proportional to the resistance of the conductor. In simpler terms, if you increase the voltage, you increase the current, provided the resistance remains constant. Conversely, if you increase the resistance while keeping the voltage the same, the current decreases.

Now, let's focus on what amperage specifically represents. Amperage is the measurement of the flow of electric charge in a circuit. It quantifies how many electrons are moving through a conductor, such as a wire, at any given moment. Imagine a water pipe: the voltage is akin to the pressure of the water, while the amperage is the flow rate of the water through the pipe. Just as a larger pipe can carry more water, a conductor with a higher amperage can carry more electrical charge. In practical terms, amperage tells us how much electricity is flowing in a circuit, which is crucial for understanding the power consumption of various devices.

The unit of measurement for amperage is the ampere, often abbreviated as "amp." One ampere is defined as one coulomb of charge passing through a point in a circuit in one second. To put this into perspective, consider a standard household circuit. In the United

States, most outlets are rated for 15 or 20 amps. This means that the maximum current that can safely flow through these circuits is 15 or 20 amperes, respectively. Exceeding this limit can lead to overheating and potentially cause a fire, which is why circuit breakers and fuses are essential safety devices in electrical systems. They are designed to interrupt the flow of electricity when the amperage exceeds safe levels, protecting both the wiring and the devices connected to the circuit.

Amperage is not just a number; it has real-world implications for the devices we use every day. For instance, when you plug in a toaster, the amperage rating tells you how much current the toaster will draw from the electrical supply. If a toaster is rated for 10 amps, it means that it will use 10 amps of current to operate effectively. Understanding amperage helps consumers make informed decisions about their electrical appliances, ensuring they do not overload circuits and cause electrical hazards.

Moreover, amperage plays a critical role in the design and operation of electrical systems. Engineers must consider the amperage when designing circuits to ensure they can handle the expected load without overheating. This involves selecting appropriate wire sizes, circuit breakers, and other components that can safely carry the required amperage. Different applications require different amperage levels; for example, industrial machinery may require hundreds of amps to operate, while a simple LED light might only need a fraction of an amp.

In summary, amperage is a crucial aspect of electricity that measures the flow of electric charge in a circuit. It is defined in terms of the ampere, which quantifies how much current passes through a point in a circuit over time. Understanding amperage is vital for anyone working with or around electrical systems, as it affects everything from circuit design to appliance safety. By grasping the concept of amperage, we can better appreciate the intricate workings of the electrical systems that power our modern lives, ensuring we use them safely and effectively.

What Are Lab Coats?

Lab coats are more than just a piece of clothing; they are a symbol of professionalism and safety in scientific environments. Typically made from cotton or a cotton-blend fabric, lab coats are designed to provide protection against spills, stains, and other hazardous materials that one might encounter in a laboratory setting. Their design is usually knee-length, featuring long sleeves and a front that can be buttoned or snapped closed, ensuring that the wearer's clothing underneath remains shielded from potential contaminants.

One of the primary functions of a lab coat is to safeguard the wearer from chemical splashes and spills. In laboratories, experiments often involve volatile substances, and a lab coat acts as a barrier between these hazardous materials and the skin. Additionally, lab coats are often treated with flame-retardant properties, which is crucial in environments where open flames or heat sources are present. This protective layer is essential for maintaining safety standards in various scientific fields, including chemistry, biology, and medicine.

Moreover, lab coats contribute to a sterile environment. In medical and research settings, wearing a lab coat helps minimize the transfer of bacteria and other pathogens. They are frequently laundered to ensure cleanliness, and many institutions have strict protocols regarding their use, including requiring them to be worn in specific areas only. Lab coats are often equipped with pockets, providing convenient storage for essential tools, pens, and notepads, allowing scientists and researchers to have everything they need at their fingertips.

In addition to their functional benefits, lab coats also foster a sense of identity and belonging among professionals. Wearing a lab coat signifies a commitment to the scientific method and ethical practices, reinforcing the notion that the wearer is part of a larger community dedicated to discovery and innovation.

Why Is It Difficult To Define Life?

Life, a concept that seems so simple on the surface, is intricately complex when we attempt to define it. The challenge lies not only in the multitude of forms life takes but also in the philosophical, biological, and existential dimensions that intertwine to create the very essence of what it means to be alive. At first glance, we might think of life in biological terms: organisms that grow, reproduce, respond to stimuli, and adapt to their environments. Yet, even this seemingly straightforward definition begins to unravel upon closer inspection.

Take viruses, for example. They exhibit some characteristics of life; they can reproduce, but only within a host cell. Outside of a living organism, they are inert, prompting the question: are they alive or not? This ambiguity illustrates the difficulty in establishing a clear boundary. The more we probe into the microscopic world, the more we realize that life is not a binary state but rather a spectrum. On one end, we have complex multicellular organisms, and on the other, we find entities that straddle the line between living and non-living.

Then there's the philosophical aspect. Throughout history, thinkers have grappled with the question of what it means to live. Ancient philosophers debated the nature of the soul, while modern existentialists ponder the meaning of existence itself. Is it consciousness that defines life? If so, what about beings with varying levels of awareness? Consider the debate surrounding sentience in animals. If a creature can feel pain or experience joy, does that grant it a status of life that transcends mere biological functions? The implications of such questions ripple through ethics, conservation, and our understanding of our place in the ecosystem.

Culturally, definitions of life can vary dramatically. In some traditions, life is seen as a sacred gift, imbued with purpose and interconnectedness, while in others, it is viewed through a more mechanistic lens, where existence is a series of chemical reactions. These differing perspectives complicate any attempt to converge on a universal definition. What one culture may regard as a living entity, another might dismiss entirely. The very act of defining life becomes a reflection of our values, beliefs, and understanding of the universe.

Furthermore, the advancement of technology adds another layer of complexity. With the rise of artificial intelligence and synthetic biology, we are faced with new entities that mimic life-like characteristics. Can a robot that learns and adapts to its environment be considered alive? What about genetically engineered organisms that blur the lines between natural and artificial? As we create life in laboratories, we must confront the ethical and philosophical ramifications of our definitions. Are we prepared to expand our understanding to include these new forms of existence, or will we cling to outdated notions that no longer serve us?

The scientific community itself is divided. Biologists often rely on specific criteria, such as metabolism, growth, and reproduction, to classify life. Yet, even within this framework, exceptions abound. Extremophiles, organisms that thrive in conditions previously thought uninhabitable, challenge our understanding of the environmental limits of life. The discovery of these resilient creatures forces us to reconsider what life can be and where it can exist.

In the end, the difficulty in defining life is not merely an academic exercise; it is a reflection of our ongoing quest to understand ourselves and the universe we inhabit. Each attempt to pin down the essence of life reveals more about our limitations than about the subject itself. As we explore the vast tapestry of existence, we must embrace the ambiguity and complexity that define life, recognizing that perhaps the beauty lies in the mystery itself. Life is not just a collection of biological processes; it is a profound enigma that invites us to ponder our existence, our connections, and the intricate web that binds all living things together.

What Is Xanthan Gum?

Xanthan gum is a fascinating substance that plays a critical role in the food industry and beyond. It is a polysaccharide, which means it is made up of long chains of sugar molecules. This particular gum is produced through the fermentation of sugar by a specific bacterium known as Xanthomonas campestris. This process is not only efficient but also sustainable, as it utilizes simple sugars derived from corn or sugar beets. The result is a thickening agent that has unique properties, making it a favorite among food manufacturers and chefs alike.

One of the most remarkable features of xanthan gum is its ability to create a viscous solution even in small quantities. Just a tiny amount can significantly alter the texture of a liquid, allowing it to mimic the consistency of dairy products or provide a smooth mouthfeel in sauces and dressings. This is particularly beneficial for gluten-free baking, as xanthan gum can help replicate the elasticity and structure that gluten typically provides in traditional recipes. It acts as a binding agent, giving baked goods a desirable texture that might otherwise be lacking.

Beyond the kitchen, xanthan gum has applications in various industries, including cosmetics, pharmaceuticals, and oil drilling. In cosmetics, it helps stabilize emulsions, ensuring that products like lotions and creams maintain their intended consistency. In pharmaceuticals, it can be used as a thickener in liquid medications, improving their delivery and effectiveness. In oil drilling, xanthan gum is utilized in drilling fluids to help control the viscosity and flow rate.

In summary, xanthan gum is more than just a food additive; it is a versatile compound with a wide range of applications that enhance both our culinary experiences and various industrial processes. Its unique properties make it an invaluable ingredient in modern food science and technology.

How Do Fireworks Work?

Fireworks are a spectacular display of light and sound, captivating audiences around the world during celebrations and holidays. But have you ever paused to wonder how these colorful explosions actually work? The science behind fireworks is a fascinating blend of chemistry, physics, and artistry. At their core, fireworks are essentially a combination of fuel, oxidizers, and various chemicals that produce the vibrant colors and effects we associate with these explosive displays.

To understand how fireworks work, we need to start with the basic components. The primary structure of a firework is the shell, which is typically made of cardboard or paper. Inside this shell are the pyrotechnic stars, which are small pellets containing the chemicals that create the colors. Each color results from a different metal salt. For instance, strontium salts produce red hues, barium gives off green, sodium creates yellow, and copper compounds yield blue. When these chemicals are heated, they emit light at specific wavelengths, which corresponds to the colors we see.

Now, let's talk about how these colors are ignited. Fireworks use a combination of black powder, or gunpowder, as a propellant and a fuse to ignite the mixture. When the fuse is lit, it ignites the black powder, creating a rapid expansion of gases. This explosion propels the firework shell into the air. The timing is crucial; the shell must reach a certain altitude before the pyrotechnic stars ignite to create the desired visual effect. This is achieved through a carefully calculated delay mechanism, which can involve additional fuses or electronic timing devices.

Once the firework reaches its peak height, the stars ignite, and this is where the real magic happens. The heat from the explosion excites the metal salts, causing them to emit light. The intensity and duration of the colors depend on the composition of the stars and the amount of oxidizer present. Oxidizers, such as potassium nitrate, are essential because they provide the oxygen needed for combustion. Without sufficient oxidizers, the firework would fizzle out instead of creating a vibrant explosion.

In addition to the colors, fireworks can produce various effects, such as crackling, whistling, or even the iconic "peony" or "chrysanthemum" shapes. These effects are achieved by altering the size and shape of the pyrotechnic stars, as well as incorporating additional materials. For example, adding small pieces of metal, like aluminum or magnesium, can create a crackling sound as they combust. The arrangement of the stars within the shell also plays a significant role in the final shape of the explosion. By arranging the stars in specific patterns, pyrotechnicians can create the desired visual effect, whether it's a burst of color or a trailing comet.

Safety is a critical aspect of firework design and handling. The materials used in fireworks can be volatile, and even a small mistake can lead to dangerous consequences. That's why professional pyrotechnicians undergo extensive training to ensure that fireworks are handled safely and effectively. They must understand the chemistry involved, the physics of the launch, and how to create the desired visual effects while minimizing risks.

In recent years, there has also been a growing interest in environmentally friendly fireworks. Traditional fireworks can produce harmful pollutants and noise, which can affect wildlife and people alike. As a result, some companies are developing alternatives that use less harmful chemicals or even no explosives at all, relying instead on laser displays or other technologies to create the visual spectacle without the environmental impact.

So, the next time you gaze up at the night sky, mesmerized by the bursts of color and sound, remember that there's a complex interplay of chemistry and physics at work behind those dazzling displays. From the careful selection of chemical compounds to the precise timing of ignition, the artistry of fireworks is a celebration of science as much as it is of light and beauty.

How Do Wave Pools Work?

Wave pools are fascinating engineering marvels, designed to simulate the natural rhythm of ocean waves within a controlled environment. The concept behind wave pools is to create a fun and safe space for people to enjoy the thrill of surfing, swimming, or simply playing in the water without the unpredictability of the ocean. At their core, wave pools operate on principles of hydraulics and buoyancy, utilizing technology to generate waves of varying sizes and frequencies.

To understand how wave pools work, we first need to consider their design. Most wave pools feature a large, shallow basin filled with water, often surrounded by a sloped beach-like area where visitors can relax or play. The key component of a wave pool is the wave-generating system, which can vary significantly from one pool to another. There are several methods to create waves, but the most common involve mechanical devices or pneumatic systems.

Mechanical wave generators use a series of paddles or plates that move back and forth in the water, displacing it to create waves. These paddles are typically powered by electric motors, which can be adjusted to change the speed and intensity of the waves. As the paddles push water away, they create a series of ripples that travel across the pool, building up to larger waves as they reach the deeper areas. The size and shape of the waves can be modified by altering the angle and speed of the paddles, allowing for a customizable experience depending on the pool's design and intended use.

On the other hand, pneumatic systems utilize air pressure to generate waves. In these systems, large air chambers are filled with compressed air, which is then released suddenly into the water. This burst of air creates a powerful surge that pushes water upward, forming waves that can reach impressive heights. Pneumatic wave pools often produce more dramatic waves and can be programmed to create specific wave patterns, making them popular for surfing simulations.

Another interesting aspect of wave pools is their ability to create different types of waves. For instance, some pools are designed to generate gentle, rolling waves perfect for beginners or families, while others can produce steep, powerful waves suitable for experienced surfers. This versatility is achieved through sophisticated control systems that monitor and adjust the wave-generating mechanisms in real-time. By using sensors and computer algorithms, operators can ensure a consistent wave pattern and maintain the safety of swimmers.

It's important to note that wave pools also incorporate safety features to protect users. The water depth is carefully regulated, and lifeguards are typically present to monitor the activities. Additionally, many wave pools have shallow areas for less experienced swimmers, allowing them to enjoy the water without the risk of being overwhelmed by large waves. Some facilities even offer surf lessons or designated times for surfing, ensuring that everyone can participate safely.

Beyond the thrill of riding waves, wave pools serve other purposes as well. They are often used for water sports competitions, training sessions, or even recreational activities like bodyboarding and paddleboarding. The controlled environment of a wave pool allows athletes to practice their skills without the variability of ocean conditions, making it an invaluable resource for surfers and water sports enthusiasts.

In conclusion, wave pools are an incredible blend of engineering and entertainment, allowing people to experience the joy of ocean waves in a safe and accessible way. By employing mechanical or pneumatic systems, these pools can generate a wide range of wave types, catering to different skill levels and preferences. As technology continues to evolve, we can expect wave pools to become even more sophisticated, offering new and exciting experiences for water lovers everywhere. Whether for leisure, sport, or simply a fun day out, wave pools stand as a testament to human ingenuity in recreating the beauty and excitement of the ocean.

What Is Graupel?

Graupel is a fascinating form of precipitation that often gets overlooked in discussions about weather phenomena. It's not quite snow, nor is it sleet or hail; graupel occupies a unique niche in the world of meteorology. To understand what graupel is, we must first consider its formation. Graupel occurs when supercooled water droplets in the atmosphere come into contact with snowflakes. These droplets freeze upon contact, creating a soft, white, pellet-like structure that resembles tiny balls of snow. This process is known as riming, and it's what gives graupel its distinct texture and appearance.

Unlike snowflakes, which are delicate and intricate, graupel is characterized by its soft, rounded shape. When you hold it in your hand, it feels almost spongy, and it can easily compress. This is because graupel is made up of many tiny ice crystals that have clumped together, forming a more solid mass than individual snowflakes. Graupel typically falls during winter storms, often in conjunction with other types of precipitation. It can occur when the temperature is just right, often hovering around freezing, creating the perfect conditions for those supercooled droplets to form.

In terms of its impact, graupel is generally not as damaging as hail, but it can still create slippery conditions on roads and sidewalks. It's often confused with snow, but it tends to be heavier and can accumulate quickly. While it may not receive the same attention as other weather phenomena, graupel plays a crucial role in the ecosystem, contributing to the overall water cycle. Its unique characteristics make it an interesting subject of study for meteorologists and weather enthusiasts alike. So, the next time you see those little white pellets falling from the sky, remember: that's graupel, a remarkable and often misunderstood form of precipitation.

What Does "Let Sleeping Dogs Lie" Mean?

The phrase "let sleeping dogs lie" is an idiom that carries a depth of meaning, often rooted in the wisdom of experience. At its core, it suggests that one should avoid stirring up trouble or revisiting past conflicts that have settled, much like a dog that is peacefully sleeping. The imagery is vivid; a dog resting comfortably poses no threat, but disturbing it can lead to unexpected consequences. This idiom serves as a cautionary reminder to tread carefully around sensitive issues or unresolved matters.

Historically, the expression can be traced back to various cultures and languages, reflecting a universal understanding of the potential dangers of provoking a dormant situation. The earliest recorded use in English dates back to the 14th century, found in Geoffrey Chaucer's work, where it was used to highlight the wisdom of leaving things undisturbed. Over the centuries, it has evolved into a common piece of advice, applicable in numerous contexts, from personal relationships to professional environments.

In relationships, whether familial, platonic, or romantic, the advice to let sleeping dogs lie can be particularly salient. Consider a situation where a couple has had a disagreement. If one partner decides to revisit the argument, perhaps to seek closure or express lingering feelings, it can reignite old wounds. The initial conflict may have seemed resolved, but bringing it back to the surface can lead to renewed tension, misunderstandings, or even a complete breakdown in communication. Thus, the phrase serves as a reminder that sometimes, it's better to leave certain issues in the past, allowing both parties to move forward without the baggage of unresolved disputes.

In the workplace, the idiom takes on a slightly different shade of meaning. Imagine a team that has successfully navigated a challenging project. If a manager decides to revisit the difficulties faced during that project, it could undermine the team's morale and accomplishments. Rather than focusing on past struggles, it is often more productive to acknowledge the success and build on it. In this context, letting sleeping dogs lie encourages a focus on progress and positivity, rather than dwelling on obstacles that have already been overcome.

Moreover, the idiom also speaks to the nature of conflict itself. In many cases, unresolved issues can fester and grow, leading to greater problems down the line. By choosing to let sleeping dogs lie, individuals can prevent minor disagreements from escalating into major conflicts. This is especially relevant in social or political discourse, where revisiting contentious topics can polarize opinions and create divisions. The wisdom here lies in recognizing that some issues might be better left undisturbed, allowing for a more harmonious coexistence.

However, it's essential to understand that letting sleeping dogs lie does not mean ignoring problems altogether. There are instances where addressing issues is crucial for growth and understanding. The key is discernment—knowing when to engage and when to step back. It requires a certain level of emotional intelligence to evaluate the potential outcomes of revisiting a topic. Sometimes, the risk of disturbance outweighs the benefits of resolution, while at other times, confronting a sleeping dog may be necessary for healing and progress.

In essence, "let sleeping dogs lie" is not merely a phrase; it encapsulates a philosophy of wisdom and caution. It encourages individuals to reflect on the implications of their actions and the potential ramifications of reopening old wounds. This idiom serves as a guiding principle, reminding us that peace often lies in acceptance and restraint. By recognizing when to engage and when to allow things to rest, we can navigate the complexities of human relationships and interactions with greater grace and understanding. In a world that often pushes us to confront every issue head-on, this wisdom remains timeless, urging us to choose our battles wisely.

What Is Gonzo Journalism?

Gonzo journalism is a style of journalism that blurs the lines between fact and fiction, often immersing the journalist in the story they are covering. It originated in the late 1960s, primarily associated with the American journalist Hunter S. Thompson, who is often considered the father of this unique form of reporting. Unlike traditional journalism, which strives for objectivity and detachment, gonzo journalism embraces subjectivity and personal experience, allowing the writer to become an integral part of the narrative. This approach challenges the conventional norms of reporting, where the journalist is expected to maintain a distance from the events they are documenting.

At its core, gonzo journalism is about authenticity and rawness. It captures the chaotic essence of human experience, often reflecting the tumultuous social and political landscape of the time. Thompson's work, particularly in "Fear and Loathing in Las Vegas," exemplifies this style. Instead of merely reporting on events, he plunged headfirst into the madness of the counterculture movement, using his own experiences, emotions, and perceptions to convey the atmosphere of the era. This method allows readers to feel as if they are experiencing the events alongside the journalist, creating a visceral connection that traditional journalism often lacks.

One of the defining characteristics of gonzo journalism is its unabashed embrace of the writer's voice. This style is marked by a conversational tone, vivid imagery, and a sense of humor, often laced with irony and sarcasm. The writer's personality shines through, making the narrative not just a recounting of events but a reflection of the author's thoughts and feelings. This personal touch can engage readers on a deeper level, inviting them to consider the complexities of the issues being discussed rather than simply absorbing information. It's this blend of personal narrative and investigative reporting that sets gonzo journalism apart.

Moreover, gonzo journalism often involves a level of immersion that goes beyond mere observation. The journalist may partake in the events they are covering, whether that means attending a political rally, participating in a protest, or even engaging in the substance use that often accompanies the subjects they are exploring. This active involvement can lead to a more nuanced understanding of the story, as the journalist experiences the highs and lows firsthand. However, this approach has its critics, who argue that such involvement can compromise the integrity of the reporting, leading to bias and a lack of objectivity.

Another aspect of gonzo journalism is its willingness to tackle taboo subjects and explore the darker sides of society. It often shines a light on issues that mainstream media may shy away from, such as drug culture, political corruption, and social injustice. By diving into these controversial topics, gonzo journalists challenge societal norms and provoke thought, encouraging readers to question their own beliefs and assumptions. This fearless exploration of uncomfortable truths is a hallmark of the gonzo style, pushing the boundaries of what journalism can be.

In recent years, the principles of gonzo journalism have found new life in the digital age, where social media and online platforms allow for even greater immediacy and personal expression. Bloggers and independent journalists now have the tools to share their experiences and insights in real-time, often adopting a gonzo approach to engage their audiences. This evolution reflects a growing desire for authenticity in journalism, as readers increasingly seek out voices that resonate with their own experiences and perspectives.

Ultimately, gonzo journalism is not just a style but a philosophy that challenges the status quo of reporting. It invites readers to step into the chaotic world of the storyteller, offering a unique lens through which to view the complexities of modern life. By intertwining personal narrative with investigative rigor, gonzo journalism creates a rich tapestry of human experience, reminding us that the truth is often as messy and multifaceted as the lives we lead. In a landscape where information is abundant but often sanitized, gonzo journalism stands as a bold testament to the power of personal narrative in understanding the world around us.

What Is A Damsel In Distress?

The term "damsel in distress" evokes images of a frail maiden, often trapped in a tower or perilously dangling from the edge of a cliff, awaiting the arrival of a gallant hero to rescue her. This archetype, deeply embedded in literature and popular culture, has roots that stretch back centuries, evolving through various narratives to reflect societal values and gender dynamics. But what exactly does it mean to be a "damsel in distress," and how has this concept influenced our understanding of gender roles and storytelling?

At its core, the damsel in distress is a narrative device that serves to highlight the vulnerability of women within a story. Traditionally, she is portrayed as passive, her fate resting squarely in the hands of the male protagonist. This trope can be traced back to medieval literature, where tales of knights and chivalry often featured young women who needed saving from dragons or wicked sorcerers. The damsel's predicament is not merely a plot point; it reflects a broader cultural perspective that often relegated women to subordinate roles, emphasizing their need for protection and rescue.

However, the damsel in distress is not just a relic of the past. She has transformed and adapted to contemporary narratives, appearing in various forms across different media. In fairy tales, she might be locked away in a castle, while in modern films, she could be a kidnapped heiress or a scientist caught in a dangerous situation. Regardless of the context, the underlying theme remains the same: the damsel is in peril and requires a hero to liberate her. This dynamic raises significant questions about agency and empowerment.

Critics of the damsel in distress trope argue that it perpetuates harmful stereotypes, reinforcing the notion that women are inherently weak and incapable of saving themselves. This portrayal can be damaging, as it suggests that women's value is tied to their relationship with men, often reducing them to mere plot devices rather than fully realized characters with their own ambitions and strengths. In essence, the damsel in distress can serve as a mirror reflecting societal attitudes toward gender, revealing an underlying belief that women are primarily defined by their vulnerability and need for male intervention.

Yet, the narrative landscape is shifting. In recent years, there has been a growing movement toward more complex and empowered female characters. The emergence of strong women who can stand on their own, face challenges, and take control of their destinies marks a significant departure from the traditional damsel. Films and literature are beginning to feature heroines who are not just waiting for rescue but are actively engaged in their own stories, showcasing resilience, intelligence, and bravery. This evolution is not merely a trend but a necessary response to the call for more diverse and realistic representations of women.

Moreover, the concept of the damsel in distress can also be reinterpreted. Some modern narratives subvert the trope by presenting characters who initially fit the damsel mold but ultimately reveal their strength and capability. These stories emphasize that vulnerability does not equate to weakness; rather, it can be a part of a broader journey of self-discovery and empowerment. By allowing female characters to experience challenges and grow from them, writers can create richer, more nuanced portrayals that resonate with contemporary audiences.

In conclusion, the damsel in distress is a multifaceted trope that has evolved over time, reflecting changing societal views on gender and agency. While it has historically reinforced stereotypes of female passivity, the narrative landscape is shifting toward more empowered representations of women. As we continue to explore and critique this archetype, it becomes essential to recognize the importance of diverse voices and stories that challenge the traditional notions of heroism and vulnerability. The damsel in distress may still appear in our narratives, but the stories we tell about her are changing, offering a more complex and empowering vision of women's experiences.

What Is Gallows Humor?

Gallows humor, often described as a form of dark or morbid humor, serves as a coping mechanism in the face of grim realities. It's a peculiar blend of laughter and discomfort, where the absurdity of life's harshest moments is met with a sardonic chuckle. This type of humor emerges from the depths of human experience, particularly in situations where fear, suffering, or death loom large. It's not merely about making jokes in inappropriate contexts; it's about finding a semblance of lightness in the darkest corners of existence.

At its core, gallows humor is rooted in the human instinct to confront the inevitable. When faced with mortality or tragedy, people often turn to humor as a shield. It's a way to reclaim some power over situations that feel overwhelmingly bleak. For instance, consider the soldier in the trenches during World War I, who cracks jokes about the grim realities surrounding him. In those moments, laughter becomes a survival tool, a way to bond with comrades and alleviate the crushing weight of fear. This phenomenon is not limited to war; it permeates various fields, including medicine, where healthcare professionals often use gallows humor to cope with the emotional toll of their work. Doctors and nurses, confronted daily with life-and-death scenarios, may share dark jokes to lighten the atmosphere, creating a sense of camaraderie in the face of adversity.

The origins of the term "gallows humor" can be traced back to the literal gallows, where condemned prisoners would often make light of their impending doom. The idea is that when one is faced with certain death, the absurdity of the situation can provoke laughter, even if it's tinged with sadness. This humor, while it may seem callous to outsiders, serves a profound purpose for those within the situation. It allows individuals to process their fears, confront their mortality, and, in some cases, find solace in shared experiences.

However, gallows humor is not universally accepted. The line between humor and insensitivity can be razor-thin, and what one person finds amusing, another may find deeply offensive. This dichotomy often sparks debates about the appropriateness of such jokes in various contexts. For example, jokes about illness or tragedy can be seen as a way to trivialize the suffering of others, leading to accusations of insensitivity. Yet, for those who have experienced similar hardships, gallows humor can feel like a lifeline, a way to connect with others who understand the gravity of the situation.

Moreover, the effectiveness of gallows humor often hinges on the relationship between the speaker and the audience. In a close-knit group, shared experiences can foster an environment where dark jokes are welcomed and appreciated. In contrast, in a more diverse or unfamiliar setting, the same jokes might fall flat or even provoke outrage. This highlights the importance of context in the realm of humor. It's not just about the content of the joke; it's also about who is telling it and to whom it is being told.

Gallows humor also serves as a reflection of cultural attitudes toward death and suffering. In some cultures, discussing death openly and humorously is accepted, while in others, it remains a taboo subject. This cultural lens shapes how individuals engage with gallows humor and informs their perceptions of mortality. In societies where death is a frequent topic of conversation, humor can act as a bridge, facilitating discussions that might otherwise be uncomfortable.

In summary, gallows humor is a complex, multifaceted phenomenon that intertwines with human psychology, culture, and social dynamics. It offers a unique perspective on the human condition, revealing our innate desire to confront fear and suffering with laughter.

While it may not be everyone's cup of tea, for many, it provides a necessary outlet, a reminder that even in the face of despair, there can still be a flicker of light—a moment where laughter dances on the edge of darkness.

What Are Some Theater Superstitions?

Theater has always been a world steeped in tradition, creativity, and a few quirks that seem to defy logic. Among these quirks, theater superstitions stand out, woven into the very fabric of the performing arts. They are peculiar practices and beliefs that have been passed down through generations, often rooted in history, folklore, and the very nature of live performance. Understanding these superstitions not only gives us insight into the mindset of performers but also highlights the unique culture that surrounds the stage.

One of the most well-known superstitions is the infamous "Macbeth curse." It's said that mentioning the title of Shakespeare's play within a theater brings bad luck. Actors and crew members will often refer to it as "the Scottish play" or "that play" to avoid invoking the curse. The origins of this superstition are murky, but many believe it stems from the play's dark themes and the fact that it has been associated with a series of unfortunate events throughout history. From accidents during performances to the deaths of cast members, the tales surrounding this curse have solidified its place as one of the theater's most enduring superstitions.

Another common belief is the idea that saying "good luck" before a performance is a jinx. Instead, performers often wish each other "break a leg." This phrase is thought to have originated from the notion that wishing someone good luck directly would invite misfortune. Instead, by wishing someone to "break a leg," it implies that they will perform so well that they will have to take a bow, thus "breaking" the leg of the stage. This phrase has become a staple in the theater community, a way to convey encouragement while sidestepping the potential for bad luck.

The color green is also steeped in superstition within the theater. Wearing green costumes is often avoided because it is believed to bring misfortune. The roots of this belief may trace back to the 19th century when green dyes were known to be unstable and could cause costumes to deteriorate quickly. Additionally, the color green has been associated with jealousy and envy, further contributing to its negative connotations. Some theaters even go so far as to ban the color entirely, opting for safer alternatives to ensure a smooth performance.

Another curious superstition involves the use of mirrors. It is commonly believed that bringing a mirror into the dressing room can attract bad luck. This superstition likely stems from the idea that mirrors can reflect energy, and in the high-stress environment of theater, negative energy can easily manifest. To avoid this, many performers prefer to keep mirrors out of their dressing areas, opting instead for a more focused and positive atmosphere as they prepare for their roles.

The act of whistling backstage is also frowned upon. This superstition likely has its roots in the days of old when stagehands would communicate using whistles. If an actor were to whistle, it could inadvertently signal a cue, leading to chaos on stage. As a result, whistling became associated with disruption and misfortune, and many theaters have adopted a strict no-whistling policy backstage.

Finally, let's not overlook the tradition of the "ghost light." This solitary bulb left burning on stage when the theater is dark serves a dual purpose: it prevents accidents by illuminating the space and is believed to appease any spirits that might linger in the theater. Many theaters have a rich history, and it's not uncommon for them to have ghost stories that accompany their performances. The ghost light acts as both a practical safety measure and a nod to the supernatural, bridging the gap between the living and the spirits of the past.

In conclusion, theater superstitions are an intriguing blend of history, belief, and the unique culture that defines the performing arts. They serve as a reminder of the delicate balance between creativity and the unpredictable nature of live performance. While some may dismiss these beliefs as mere folklore, for those who step onto the stage, they are an integral part of the experience, shaping the rituals and traditions that make theater such a captivating and enduring art form.

What Are Rose-Colored Glasses?

Rose-colored glasses, a phrase often used to describe an optimistic or overly positive outlook on life, originates from the literal use of tinted lenses that soften the harshness of reality. When someone wears rose-colored glasses, they perceive the world through a lens that alters their view, making everything appear more pleasant and beautiful than it might actually be. This metaphorical eyewear symbolizes a mindset that chooses to focus on the bright side, often ignoring the darker aspects of life.

Historically, the phrase has deep roots in literature and culture, often associated with the naive optimism of youth or an idealistic perspective that may not align with reality. It suggests a willingness to overlook flaws, either in oneself or in the world, in favor of a more cheerful interpretation. While this can foster a sense of hope and positivity, it can also lead to disillusionment when faced with the inevitable challenges of life.

Psychologically, wearing rose-colored glasses can be both a defense mechanism and a coping strategy. It can provide comfort in difficult times, allowing individuals to maintain a sense of hope and resilience. However, it can also hinder personal growth by preventing one from confronting uncomfortable truths. When people refuse to acknowledge the reality of their circumstances, they risk becoming unprepared for the challenges that lie ahead.

In relationships, wearing rose-colored glasses can lead to unrealistic expectations. Individuals may overlook red flags or dismiss serious issues in favor of a more idyllic view of their partner. While optimism can enrich relationships, it's essential to balance it with a realistic perspective to foster genuine connection and understanding.

Ultimately, rose-colored glasses represent a choice—one that can bring joy but also demands a careful examination of the world as it truly is, not just how we wish it to be.

What Is The Difference Between A Team And A Group?

When we talk about teams and groups, we often use the terms interchangeably, thinking they mean the same thing. However, there's a significant difference between the two, and understanding this distinction can enhance our interactions in both personal and professional settings. At the core, the primary difference lies in the structure, purpose, and dynamics of how individuals come together.

A group is often defined as a collection of individuals who come together, but not necessarily with a common goal. Think of it as a gathering of people who happen to be in the same place at the same time. They may share a common interest, like a book club, or they might be colleagues working in the same department, but their collaboration is usually limited. Members of a group may work independently, with each person focusing on their own tasks without a strong reliance on one another. There's a sense of individualism in a group; each person is responsible for their own contributions, and there's less emphasis on the collective outcome.

In contrast, a team is a more cohesive unit. A team is built on a foundation of shared objectives and interdependence. Members of a team work collaboratively towards a common goal, leveraging each other's strengths and compensating for weaknesses. In a team, the success of one member directly influences the success of the whole. This interdependence creates a dynamic where communication and collaboration are crucial. Team members engage in discussions, share ideas, and provide support to one another. They understand that their individual efforts contribute to a larger purpose, and this fosters a sense of accountability and commitment.

Another key difference is in the nature of leadership within groups and teams. Groups often have a more informal structure, and leadership can be fluid or even absent. In a group, individuals may take turns leading discussions or projects, but there's no designated leader guiding the group towards a specific outcome. In contrast, teams typically have defined roles and responsibilities, often with a designated leader who facilitates collaboration, sets goals, and monitors progress. This leader plays a vital role in ensuring that the team remains focused and motivated, helping to navigate challenges and celebrate successes together.

Moreover, the dynamics of interaction differ significantly between groups and teams. In a group, interactions can be superficial; members may engage in small talk or surface-level discussions without delving deeper into the issues at hand. There's often less accountability for participation, and some individuals may choose to disengage entirely. In a team, however, the interactions are more profound and meaningful. Team members challenge each other's ideas, provide constructive feedback, and work through conflicts collaboratively. This level of engagement fosters trust and respect, creating a safe environment for creativity and innovation.

Let's also consider the outcomes. Groups may achieve results, but these results are often fragmented and less impactful. The focus is on individual accomplishments rather than collective success. Teams, however, are designed to achieve specific goals, and their outcomes are often more significant and far-reaching. The synergy created by working closely together allows teams to produce results that exceed what any individual could accomplish alone.

In summary, while both teams and groups consist of individuals coming together, the differences in their structure, purpose, leadership, interaction, and outcomes are profound. Groups are collections of individuals with varying degrees of interaction and commitment, while teams are cohesive units working collaboratively towards a common goal. Understanding these differences is crucial for anyone looking to foster effective collaboration, whether in a workplace, a community organization, or any other setting where people come together. Recognizing the unique strengths of teams can lead to more productive and satisfying experiences, ultimately driving success in our collective endeavors.

What Is Schadenfreude?

Schadenfreude, a term that rolls off the tongue with a peculiar blend of elegance and mischief, originates from the German language, where "Schaden" means harm and "Freude" means joy. It encapsulates a complex and often uncomfortable emotion—the pleasure derived from another person's misfortune. At its core, schadenfreude is a fascinating reflection of human nature, revealing the intricacies of our emotional responses to the successes and failures of those around us. It's a sentiment that many experience but few openly acknowledge, a guilty pleasure that lurks in the shadows of our conscience.

To understand schadenfreude fully, one must first explore its psychological underpinnings. Research suggests that this emotion often arises in competitive contexts, where individuals compare themselves to others. When someone we perceive as a rival stumbles or faces adversity, it can trigger a sense of relief or even delight within us. This reaction is not merely a reflection of malice; it often stems from a desire to elevate our own self-worth. In moments of insecurity, witnessing another's downfall can provide a fleeting sense of superiority, a balm for our own insecurities. This dynamic is particularly evident in social media culture, where the public lives of others are laid bare, and the schadenfreude response is amplified by the constant comparison we engage in.

Interestingly, schadenfreude is not limited to personal rivalries; it can also extend to public figures and celebrities. When a beloved icon faces scandal or failure, there's a collective gasp followed by a wave of commentary that often veers into the realm of delight. This phenomenon raises questions about our collective morality. Are we reveling in their downfall because we feel they deserve it, or is it simply a reflection of our own frustrations and disappointments? The answer is likely a mix of both. We may feel justified in our pleasure, believing that the universe has balanced the scales, that those who seem untouchable have finally faced their comeuppance.

Yet, schadenfreude is not always a negative emotion. It can serve as a coping mechanism, a way to process our feelings about the unpredictability of life. When we see someone else falter, it can remind us of our own vulnerabilities, humanizing the experience of failure. It's a reminder that no one is immune to hardship, that the façade of perfection is often just that—a façade. In this way, schadenfreude can foster a sense of connection, a shared understanding of the trials of existence. It can allow us to laugh at the absurdity of life's challenges, to find humor in our shared human experience.

However, it is crucial to approach schadenfreude with caution. While it can be a natural response, indulging in it too freely can lead to a toxic mindset. When we become too invested in the misfortunes of others, we risk losing sight of our own empathy and compassion. The line between healthy amusement and harmful glee can blur, leading us to revel in the pain of others rather than learning from it. It can create a cycle of negativity, where we become so focused on others' failures that we neglect our own growth and happiness.

In conclusion, schadenfreude is a complex emotion that reflects the multifaceted nature of human psychology. It serves as a mirror, revealing our insecurities, our desires for validation, and our need for connection. While it can provide a momentary sense of joy, it also challenges us to examine our values and the way we relate to others. As we navigate our lives, it's essential to acknowledge this emotion without letting it define us. Embracing our shared humanity, understanding that we all stumble and fall, can lead to a more compassionate perspective—one that allows us to find joy not just in the misfortunes of others, but also in our collective resilience.

What Is The Fog Of War?

The Fog of War is a term that evokes a multitude of images and emotions, often conjuring up thoughts of chaos, confusion, and the unpredictable nature of conflict. At its core, the Fog of War refers to the uncertainty and ambiguity that surrounds military operations. It encapsulates the idea that in the midst of battle, clarity is often obscured, making it difficult for commanders and soldiers alike to make informed decisions. This concept has been studied extensively through the lens of history, strategy, and psychology, revealing profound insights into the nature of warfare and human behavior.

Historically, the term gained prominence through the writings of military theorist Carl von Clausewitz, who articulated the complexities of war in his seminal work, "On War." Clausewitz argued that war is not merely a series of battles but a dynamic interplay of chance, friction, and the unpredictable actions of adversaries. The Fog of War highlights how information can be incomplete or misleading, leading to miscalculations and strategic blunders. This uncertainty can stem from various sources: the fog of battle itself, the fog of misinformation, and even the fog of one's own limitations in understanding the enemy's intentions and capabilities.

In practical terms, the Fog of War manifests in several ways during military engagements. For instance, commanders may struggle to obtain accurate intelligence about enemy positions, troop movements, or logistical capabilities. This lack of clarity can lead to poorly informed decisions, such as launching an attack when the enemy is better positioned or failing to anticipate a counteroffensive. The chaos of battle can further complicate matters, as the noise, smoke, and confusion can distort perceptions and hinder effective communication among troops. Soldiers on the ground may find themselves navigating a landscape fraught with uncertainty, where the enemy's actions are unpredictable and the terrain itself can shift in an instant.

Moreover, the Fog of War is not limited to external factors; it also encompasses the internal struggles faced by military leaders. The pressure of command, the weight of responsibility, and the ethical dilemmas inherent in warfare can cloud judgment. Leaders must grapple with their own biases and assumptions, which can further obscure their understanding of the situation. The psychological toll of combat can lead to panic, hesitation, or overconfidence, all of which can have dire consequences on the battlefield.

In the modern context, the Fog of War has evolved with advancements in technology and warfare. The introduction of drones, cyber warfare, and real-time intelligence has transformed the landscape of conflict. While these tools can provide greater clarity and precision, they also introduce new layers of complexity. The sheer volume of information available can be overwhelming, leading to what some call "information overload." Commanders must now sift through vast amounts of data, discerning what is relevant and actionable amidst the noise. The challenge of interpreting this information accurately is a modern manifestation of the Fog of War.

The implications of the Fog of War extend beyond the battlefield. Understanding this concept is crucial for policymakers, military strategists, and historians alike. It serves as a reminder that decisions made in the heat of conflict are often fraught with uncertainty and risk. This understanding can inform more cautious and nuanced approaches to military engagement, emphasizing the importance of thorough preparation, adaptable strategies, and the need for robust intelligence-gathering mechanisms.

In conclusion, the Fog of War is a multifaceted concept that encapsulates the inherent uncertainty of military conflict. It challenges our perceptions of control and clarity in the face of chaos, urging us to recognize the complexities of decision-making in warfare. As we reflect on the lessons of history and the evolving nature of conflict, acknowledging the Fog of War can lead to a deeper understanding of the human experience in times of crisis, reminding us that clarity is often a luxury that eludes us in the tumult of battle.

What Does "Light At The End Of The Tunnel" Mean?

The phrase "light at the end of the tunnel" is a metaphor that has woven itself into the fabric of our language, resonating with anyone who has faced adversity or hardship. It evokes a sense of hope, a glimmer of promise amid darkness. But what does it truly mean? At its core, this expression signifies the idea that after enduring a difficult period, relief or resolution is on the horizon. It captures the universal human experience of struggling through challenges, whether they are personal, emotional, or situational, and the innate desire to emerge into a brighter, more hopeful future.

Historically, the phrase can be traced back to the literal experience of traveling through tunnels, where the darkness can feel all-consuming. As one progresses through the tunnel, the faint light at the end serves as a beacon, a reminder that the journey, however daunting, will eventually lead to a place of safety and clarity. This imagery resonates deeply because it mirrors our own struggles. Life is often akin to navigating a long, dark tunnel; the path can be fraught with obstacles, uncertainties, and fears. It is in these moments of despair that the notion of light becomes most significant.

Psychologically, the concept of light at the end of the tunnel plays a crucial role in how we cope with stress and adversity. When faced with challenges, maintaining a sense of hope can be a powerful motivator. Research in psychology suggests that hope is linked to resilience. Resilient individuals are often those who can envision a positive outcome, who can see that light, no matter how dim it may be. This hope acts as a psychological buffer, helping to mitigate feelings of helplessness and despair. It encourages us to keep moving forward, to persist in the face of difficulties, and to seek out solutions rather than succumb to negativity.

In practical terms, the phrase can be applied to various aspects of life. In health, for instance, patients undergoing treatment for chronic illnesses often find themselves in a metaphorical tunnel. The journey can be grueling, filled with pain, uncertainty, and fear of the unknown. Yet, many hold onto the belief that there will be a resolution, that they will emerge healthier and stronger. The light at the end of the tunnel becomes a symbol of recovery, a promise of better days ahead.

In the realm of personal relationships, the phrase can signify the hope of reconciliation after conflict. Relationships often go through tumultuous phases, where misunderstandings and disagreements can create a chasm of darkness. However, with communication, empathy, and effort, couples can find their way back to each other, rediscovering the light that once illuminated their connection. The journey through that darkness can be challenging, but the light signifies the potential for healing and renewal.

Moreover, in the context of societal challenges, such as economic downturns or social injustices, the light at the end of the tunnel represents collective hope for change. Communities facing adversity often rally together, believing in the possibility of a brighter future. Movements for social justice, environmental sustainability, and economic reform are fueled by the shared vision of a better world. The light symbolizes progress, the potential for transformation that lies ahead if people come together and work toward a common goal.

In conclusion, the phrase "light at the end of the tunnel" encapsulates a profound truth about the human experience. It reminds us that no matter how daunting the challenges we face may seem, there is always the possibility of hope, healing, and resolution. It encourages us to persevere, to seek out the light even when it feels distant, and to believe in the promise of a brighter tomorrow. Ultimately, it is this belief that propels us forward, guiding us through the darkest tunnels of our lives toward the illuminating light that awaits us.

What Is Conditioned Helplessness?

Conditioned helplessness is a psychological phenomenon that arises when an individual learns to believe that their actions have no impact on their circumstances, often due to repeated exposure to uncontrollable and adverse events. This concept was first identified in the 1960s by psychologists Martin Seligman and Steven Maier through experiments with dogs. They discovered that animals could be conditioned to feel helpless, even when escape was possible. In these experiments, dogs were exposed to electric shocks in a situation where they could not escape. Over time, they learned to accept their fate, even when given the opportunity to escape the shocks in later trials. This learned helplessness can be extended to humans, manifesting in various ways, such as depression, anxiety, and a general sense of powerlessness.

When individuals experience uncontrollable events, they may begin to internalize the belief that their actions are futile. This can lead to a cycle of inaction, where they stop trying to change their situation, reinforcing the belief that they are powerless. For example, a student who fails an exam despite studying hard may conclude that no amount of effort will lead to success, resulting in disengagement from future academic pursuits. Similarly, someone in an abusive relationship may feel trapped, believing that their attempts to escape will only lead to further suffering.

Conditioned helplessness can also have broader societal implications. It can perpetuate cycles of poverty, discrimination, and mental health issues, as individuals feel they lack control over their lives. However, understanding this concept is crucial for breaking the cycle. By recognizing the signs of conditioned helplessness, individuals can seek help, develop coping strategies, and regain a sense of agency, ultimately transforming their outlook and reclaiming their power in the face of adversity.

What Is A Non-Sequitur?

A non-sequitur is a term that originates from Latin, meaning "it does not follow." In the context of logic and rhetoric, a non-sequitur refers to a statement or conclusion that does not logically follow from the previous argument or statement. It's like a jigsaw puzzle piece that doesn't fit into the picture, creating confusion rather than clarity. Imagine you're having a conversation about the weather, and suddenly someone declares that they prefer chocolate ice cream. That's a non-sequitur; it's an unexpected leap that disrupts the flow of dialogue and leaves everyone scratching their heads.

Non-sequiturs can appear in everyday conversation, literature, and even formal arguments. They can be used intentionally for comedic effect, creating absurdity that elicits laughter. Think of a stand-up comedian who tells a story about their day at the park and then abruptly shifts to a bizarre claim about how bananas are plotting to take over the world. The humor arises from the unexpected nature of the statement, which stands in stark contrast to the preceding narrative. However, non-sequiturs can also be unintentional and may indicate a lack of coherence in thought or speech. When someone makes a non-sequitur in a serious discussion, it can undermine their credibility and confuse the audience.

In logic, non-sequiturs are categorized as fallacies, specifically as a failure in reasoning. They can manifest in various forms, such as affirming the consequent or denying the antecedent. For instance, if someone argues that because it is raining, the streets are wet, and then concludes that the streets must have been washed, they are committing a non-sequitur. The conclusion does not follow logically from the premises; there could be other explanations for the wet streets. This kind of faulty reasoning can lead to misunderstandings and flawed arguments, making it crucial to recognize and avoid them in serious discourse.

In literature, non-sequiturs can serve as a stylistic device, often found in absurdist works or surrealist narratives. Authors like Lewis Carroll and Samuel Beckett employed non-sequiturs to challenge conventional logic and provoke thought. In "Alice's Adventures in Wonderland," for instance, the characters frequently engage in nonsensical exchanges that defy rational explanation, creating a dreamlike atmosphere that reflects the absurdity of life itself. These non-sequitur moments invite readers to question the boundaries of logic and reality, encouraging a deeper exploration of meaning beyond the surface.

In political discourse, non-sequiturs can be particularly dangerous. Politicians or public figures may use them to divert attention from a pressing issue or to manipulate the audience's perception. For example, during a debate about healthcare, a politician might suddenly pivot to discussing their favorite sports team. This tactic can distract from the original topic, allowing them to avoid addressing uncomfortable questions or criticisms. Recognizing non-sequiturs in such contexts is essential for critical thinking and informed decision-making, as it helps to identify when arguments are being obfuscated or when the focus is being shifted away from important issues.

Ultimately, understanding non-sequiturs enhances our ability to engage in meaningful conversation and critical analysis. They remind us of the importance of coherence and logic in our communication. Whether in casual discussions, literary interpretations, or political debates, being aware of non-sequiturs allows us to navigate the complexities of language and thought more effectively. It encourages us to seek clarity and connection in our exchanges, fostering deeper understanding and engagement with the world around us. So next time you encounter a statement that leaves you puzzled, take a moment to consider whether it's a non-sequitur, and reflect on the implications it carries for the conversation at hand.

What Is An Ad Hominem Attack?

An ad hominem attack is a term frequently encountered in discussions about logic, debate, and rhetoric, yet many people may not fully grasp its implications or significance. At its core, an ad hominem attack refers to a specific type of logical fallacy where an argument is rebutted by attacking the character or personal traits of the individual making the argument, rather than addressing the substance of the argument itself. This tactic can be particularly insidious because it shifts the focus away from the actual issue at hand, diverting attention to irrelevant personal characteristics instead.

The term "ad hominem" is derived from Latin, meaning "to the person." This phrase encapsulates the essence of the fallacy: instead of engaging with the argument presented, the attacker opts to undermine the credibility of the person making that argument. For instance, if someone argues for the importance of environmental conservation and their opponent counters by pointing out that they once drove a gas-guzzling vehicle, that's an ad hominem attack. The focus has shifted from the argument about conservation to a personal attack on the individual's past choices. This type of reasoning is flawed because it does not engage with the merits of the argument itself; it merely seeks to discredit the speaker.

Ad hominem attacks can take various forms, ranging from outright insults to more subtle insinuations. A common example might be the dismissal of a person's opinion based on their perceived lack of expertise, often referred to as "poisoning the well." For instance, if a scientist presents research on climate change and a detractor responds by highlighting the scientist's personal life or unrelated failures, this is not only disrespectful but also a failure to engage with the scientific evidence being presented. Such tactics can create a toxic environment in discussions, where individuals feel compelled to defend their character instead of their ideas.

In political discourse, ad hominem attacks are rampant. Politicians often resort to personal attacks against their opponents rather than debating policies or ideologies. This strategy can be effective in swaying public opinion, as it capitalizes on emotional responses rather than rational thought. When voters are bombarded with negative portrayals of candidates, they may find themselves more influenced by these personal narratives than by the candidates' actual platforms or qualifications.

Moreover, ad hominem attacks can perpetuate a cycle of negativity that undermines civil discourse. When one side resorts to personal attacks, the other may feel justified in responding in kind, leading to an escalation of hostility. This dynamic can stifle meaningful dialogue and prevent the exploration of important issues. Instead of fostering understanding and collaboration, discussions devolve into a series of personal grievances and accusations, ultimately leaving the original topic unresolved.

It is crucial to recognize ad hominem attacks not only in public debates but also in everyday conversations. They can seep into discussions about personal beliefs, social issues, and even casual exchanges among friends. When someone dismisses another's viewpoint by attacking their character or background, it diminishes the potential for constructive dialogue. Instead of fostering an environment where ideas can be exchanged and challenged, ad hominem tactics create barriers that hinder understanding and growth.

In conclusion, an ad hominem attack is a logical fallacy that detracts from meaningful discourse by shifting the focus from the argument to the individual making it. By recognizing and calling out these tactics, we can encourage more respectful and substantive conversations. Engaging with ideas on their merits, rather than resorting to personal attacks, fosters an environment where diverse perspectives can be shared and debated. Ultimately, the goal should be to elevate the conversation, allowing for a deeper understanding of the issues that matter most.

What Is A Pyrrhic Victory?

A Pyrrhic victory is a term that originates from the ancient world, specifically from King Pyrrhus of Epirus, who fought against the Romans in the 3rd century BCE. It refers to a victory that comes at such a significant cost to the victor that it is almost tantamount to defeat. In essence, winning the battle leaves you in a state of such loss that it undermines any sense of achievement. The term encapsulates a paradox that exists in many aspects of life, where the pursuit of success can lead to detrimental consequences that overshadow any benefits gained.

To understand this concept better, let's delve into its historical context. During the Battle of Heraclea in 280 BCE, Pyrrhus faced the Roman legions and emerged victorious. However, his army suffered heavy casualties. The same pattern repeated itself in 279 BCE at the Battle of Asculum, where he again defeated the Romans but lost a considerable number of his troops. Pyrrhus famously remarked that another such victory would ruin him. This sentiment captures the essence of a Pyrrhic victory: the notion that the cost of winning can be so high that it negates the very purpose of fighting.

In broader terms, a Pyrrhic victory can manifest in various arenas, be it in personal relationships, business, or even political endeavors. For instance, consider a corporate takeover where a company successfully acquires a competitor but incurs massive debt in the process. The short-term gain of acquiring market share is overshadowed by the long-term financial strain that results from the acquisition. The victory, while celebrated by executives, may ultimately lead to layoffs, reduced morale, and a tarnished reputation.

Similarly, in personal relationships, one might "win" an argument with a loved one but at the expense of trust and emotional connection. Winning the verbal battle can leave both parties feeling wounded, and the relationship may suffer irreparable damage. The victory feels hollow when you realize that the emotional toll outweighs the satisfaction of having been right.

In politics, a Pyrrhic victory can be observed in election campaigns. A candidate may win a contentious race but do so by alienating a significant portion of the electorate. The victory can lead to a fractured political landscape, making it difficult to govern effectively. The cost of winning can manifest in a loss of credibility, trust, and the ability to unite constituents.

The implications of a Pyrrhic victory extend beyond the immediate aftermath of a conflict or competition. It serves as a cautionary tale about the nature of success and the importance of weighing the costs associated with achieving one's goals. In a world that often glorifies victory, it is crucial to consider the broader ramifications of our actions.

Furthermore, the concept encourages a reflection on what constitutes true success. Is it merely winning, or is it about achieving a sustainable outcome that fosters growth and well-being? A Pyrrhic victory prompts us to reassess our definitions of success and consider the long-term consequences of our pursuits.

In conclusion, a Pyrrhic victory is a complex and multifaceted concept that resonates across various domains of life. It serves as a reminder that not all victories are created equal, and the costs associated with winning can sometimes render the achievement meaningless. In our quest for success, it is imperative to remain vigilant about the potential consequences of our actions and to strive for outcomes that promote overall well-being rather than fleeting triumphs. Understanding the nature of a Pyrrhic victory allows us to navigate our endeavors with a more nuanced perspective, one that values not just the destination but the journey and its impact on ourselves and those around us.

What Is A Scapegoat?

A scapegoat is a person or group that is unfairly blamed for problems, misfortunes, or negative outcomes, often to divert attention from the real issues at hand. The term originates from an ancient ritual described in the Bible, specifically in the Book of Leviticus, where a goat was symbolically burdened with the sins of the people and then sent into the wilderness, effectively carrying away their transgressions. This ritual illustrates the core idea behind scapegoating: the transfer of blame from one entity to another, allowing the original offenders to escape accountability. In modern contexts, scapegoats can be found in various social, political, and personal situations, often manifesting in ways that reveal deeper societal issues.

In many cases, scapegoating serves as a psychological defense mechanism. When individuals or groups face uncomfortable truths or failures, it can be easier to project their shortcomings onto someone else rather than confront their own flaws. This is particularly evident in group dynamics, where a collective identity can lead to the identification of an outsider or a minority as the source of problems. By designating a scapegoat, the group can unify against a common enemy, reinforcing their own identity while deflecting attention from their internal conflicts or failures. This phenomenon is not limited to interpersonal relationships; it can also be observed on a larger scale, such as in political discourse, where leaders might blame certain demographics or nations for economic downturns or social unrest.

The consequences of scapegoating can be devastating. The targeted individual or group often faces social ostracism, discrimination, and violence, all based on unfounded accusations or stereotypes. History is rife with examples of scapegoating leading to tragic outcomes, such as the persecution of Jews during the Black Death, when they were wrongfully blamed for the plague, or the internment of Japanese Americans during World War II, fueled by wartime hysteria and racial prejudice. These instances highlight the dangerous potential of scapegoating to dehumanize individuals and justify systemic injustices.

In personal relationships, scapegoating can manifest in families or among friends. A child might be blamed for a family's financial struggles, or a friend might be held responsible for a failed project, regardless of their actual contribution. This not only harms the scapegoat but also stifles honest communication and resolution of the underlying issues. It creates an environment where accountability is avoided, and growth is stunted, as the focus remains on blame rather than understanding and healing.

Scapegoating can also be perpetuated by media narratives and societal stereotypes. When certain groups are consistently portrayed in a negative light, it becomes easier for the public to accept them as scapegoats during times of crisis. For instance, immigrants are often blamed for economic woes, even when evidence suggests that they contribute positively to society. This scapegoating is reinforced by sensationalist media coverage that simplifies complex issues into digestible narratives, fostering fear and division.

Addressing the phenomenon of scapegoating requires a commitment to critical thinking and empathy. It is essential to recognize the complexities of human behavior and the multifaceted nature of societal problems. Rather than seeking a simple explanation or an easy target, we must strive to understand the underlying causes of our challenges and engage in open dialogue. This involves challenging our biases and seeking to understand the perspectives of those who are often marginalized or unfairly blamed.

Ultimately, a scapegoat is not merely a victim of circumstance; they are a reflection of our collective failures to confront the truth. By acknowledging this, we can begin to dismantle the patterns of blame and division that plague our societies, fostering a culture of accountability and understanding instead. In doing so, we not only liberate the scapegoats from their unjust burdens but also free ourselves from the shackles of ignorance and prejudice that perpetuate these harmful dynamics.

What Is A Conniption Fit?

A conniption fit, often simply referred to as a conniption, is a term that might sound amusing, but it describes a rather intense emotional response. It's a sudden outburst of anger, frustration, or excitement, often characterized by exaggerated behavior. Picture someone who has reached their breaking point, perhaps due to overwhelming stress or an unexpected inconvenience. In that moment, they might yell, flail their arms, or even throw objects, embodying the chaotic nature of the fit itself. The origins of the term are somewhat unclear, but it is believed to have emerged in the 19th century, possibly derived from the word "conniption," which suggests a kind of fit or seizure.

Conniption fits are often used in a light-hearted context, a way to describe someone who is overreacting to a situation. It's not uncommon to hear someone say, "I nearly had a conniption fit when I saw the mess in the kitchen!" This phrase captures the essence of the term, illustrating how everyday frustrations can lead to exaggerated emotional responses.

While the term itself may be humorous, it can also highlight the real struggles people face when overwhelmed. Stress and anxiety can manifest in various ways, and a conniption fit is one of those colorful expressions of human emotion. It's a reminder of our limits and the sometimes chaotic nature of our reactions. In a world that often demands perfection and composure, a conniption fit serves as a release valve, allowing us to vent our frustrations, albeit in a dramatic fashion. So, the next time you encounter someone having a conniption, remember that it's not just a fit of anger; it's a vivid expression of the human experience, a moment where emotions spill over, reminding us that we're all just trying to navigate the complexities of life.

What Is Phatic Communication?

Phatic communication, a term that may not roll off the tongue for many, is a fascinating concept in the realm of linguistics and social interaction. It refers to the type of communication that serves a social function rather than a purely informational one. Think of it as the lubricant that keeps the wheels of conversation turning, the social glue that binds people together. It's not about exchanging vital information or conveying profound thoughts; rather, it's about establishing a connection, creating a sense of belonging, or simply acknowledging another person's presence.

Consider the everyday exchanges we often overlook: the casual "How are you?" that we toss around like a frisbee, or the friendly nod to a neighbor as we pass each other on the street. These interactions may seem trivial, but they play a crucial role in our social lives. They are the verbal equivalent of a handshake or a smile, serving to reinforce social bonds and maintain relationships. In fact, phatic communication can be found in every culture and language, manifesting in various forms, from small talk to greetings, and even in silence.

The term "phatic" comes from the Greek word "phatos," meaning "spoken" or "uttered." It was popularized by the anthropologist Bronislaw Malinowski in the early 20th century, who argued that language serves different functions beyond mere information transfer. He noted that in some contexts, the act of speaking itself is what matters most. When we greet someone, we're not necessarily looking for a detailed account of their day; we're acknowledging their presence, reaffirming our connection, and fostering a sense of community.

This type of communication is particularly important in social settings. It helps break the ice in new relationships and can ease tensions in uncomfortable situations. Think about a job interview or a first date. The initial exchanges often revolve around light topics, like the weather or mutual interests, rather than diving straight into the meat of the matter. These phatic exchanges create a comfortable atmosphere, allowing both parties to feel more at ease.

Phatic communication also plays a significant role in maintaining relationships over time. Friends who haven't seen each other in a while might start their conversation with a series of "Hey, how have you been?" and "It's been so long!" before delving into deeper topics. These phatic elements are crucial; they signal that the relationship is valued, that there is a history to acknowledge, and that both parties are invested in the connection.

Interestingly, phatic communication is not limited to spoken language. Nonverbal cues, such as a wave, a smile, or even a thumbs-up, carry the same weight. In digital communication, emojis and reaction GIFs serve a similar purpose, allowing individuals to express sentiments without necessarily saying anything substantial. These forms of communication can enhance online interactions, making them feel more personal and engaging.

However, it's essential to recognize that phatic communication can also be misinterpreted. In some cultures, a simple greeting might be perceived as a genuine inquiry into one's well-being, while in others, it's merely a formality. This cultural nuance can lead to misunderstandings, highlighting the importance of context in communication.

Ultimately, phatic communication is a vital aspect of human interaction. It fosters connections, builds rapport, and creates a sense of belonging in an often chaotic world. While it may not carry the weight of profound discourse, its significance cannot be overstated. In a society that thrives on relationships, both personal and professional, understanding the nuances of phatic communication can enhance our interactions and deepen our connections with others. So, the next time you engage in small talk or offer a friendly greeting, remember that you're participating in a rich tapestry of social interaction that binds us all together. Phatic communication, in all its simplicity, is a powerful reminder of our shared humanity.

What Are Movie Posters?

Movie posters are more than just colorful advertisements plastered on walls or displayed in theaters; they are a unique blend of art, marketing, and storytelling, designed to capture the essence of a film and entice audiences to experience it. At their core, movie posters serve as visual representations of the film's themes, characters, and overall tone. They distill the essence of a movie into a single image, often accompanied by a catchy tagline or a brief synopsis, all while adhering to the conventions of graphic design and marketing strategy.

The history of movie posters dates back to the late 19th century, coinciding with the birth of cinema itself. Early posters were simple, often featuring hand-drawn illustrations or photographs of the stars. As the film industry evolved, so did the artistry and complexity of these posters. The Golden Age of Hollywood saw the emergence of iconic designs that have since become synonymous with cinema. Designers like Saul Bass and Drew Struzan revolutionized the art of poster design, creating visuals that not only promoted the films but also contributed to their cultural significance.

A movie poster's primary purpose is to communicate information about the film. This includes the title, the names of the key actors, the director, and sometimes even the genre. But beyond mere information, a successful poster conveys a mood or emotion, often through the use of color, typography, and imagery. For instance, a horror film might employ dark colors and ominous imagery to evoke fear and suspense, while a romantic comedy might use bright colors and playful fonts to suggest lightheartedness and joy. The design elements work together to create an immediate emotional response from potential viewers.

Typography plays a crucial role in movie poster design. The choice of font can communicate a lot about the film's genre and tone. Bold, sharp fonts might suggest action or intensity, while softer, rounded fonts could imply romance or comedy. Designers carefully select typefaces that not only look appealing but also resonate with the film's narrative. For example, a historical drama might use serif fonts that evoke a sense of tradition and seriousness, while a sci-fi film might lean towards sleek, modern sans-serif fonts that suggest futurism and innovation.

Imagery is another critical component of movie posters. The central image often features the film's protagonist or a key scene that encapsulates the story. This image is crafted to draw the viewer in, sparking curiosity and interest. Sometimes, posters will use a collage of images to represent various characters or plot points, creating a dynamic visual narrative that hints at the film's complexity. Iconic examples include the posters for "Jaws," which features the menacing shark looming beneath the surface, or "Star Wars," which showcases a heroic ensemble against a backdrop of space battles. These images become etched in popular culture, often transcending the films themselves.

In the digital age, the role of movie posters has expanded beyond traditional print media. Online platforms and social media have given rise to new formats and styles, allowing for animated posters or interactive designs that engage audiences in novel ways. The internet has also democratized poster design, with fans creating their own interpretations and alternative designs that can go viral, further promoting the film and generating buzz.

Despite the evolution of film marketing, the fundamental purpose of movie posters remains unchanged: to attract audiences and convey the film's essence. They are a crucial part of the cinematic experience, acting as the first point of contact for potential viewers. In a world saturated with content, a well-crafted movie poster can cut through the noise, sparking interest and anticipation. As we continue to navigate the ever-changing landscape of film and media, the artistry and significance of movie posters endure, reminding us that even in a digital world, the power of visual storytelling remains paramount.

What Are 15 Minutes Of Fame?

Fame, that elusive concept that dances just beyond our fingertips, often manifests in fleeting moments that are both exhilarating and ephemeral. The phrase "15 minutes of fame" has become a cultural touchstone, capturing the essence of how quickly recognition can rise and fall. Coined by Andy Warhol in the 1960s, this idea suggests that in a world increasingly saturated with media and information, everyone will experience a brief period of notoriety or celebrity. But what does this really mean? What are these 15 minutes of fame, and why do they matter?

To begin with, let's unpack the nature of fame itself. Fame is not merely about being well-known; it is the acknowledgment and attention received from the public. It can stem from various sources: talent, scandal, achievement, or even sheer randomness. In today's digital age, the pathways to fame have multiplied exponentially. Social media platforms, reality television, and viral trends have democratized fame, making it accessible to anyone with a smartphone and an internet connection. This accessibility has led to a phenomenon where ordinary individuals can catapult into the spotlight overnight, often for reasons that seem trivial or absurd.

Consider the viral videos that flood our feeds. One moment, a person is an anonymous face in a crowd; the next, they are a meme, a dancing sensation, or the subject of countless parodies. These instances of sudden fame can be exhilarating. They offer a rush of validation, a momentary high that can be intoxicating. However, this fleeting recognition often comes with its own set of challenges. The pressure to maintain relevance can be overwhelming. Many who experience their 15 minutes find themselves grappling with the question of how to extend that moment, how to parlay a brief burst of attention into something more sustainable.

Moreover, the nature of modern fame is often superficial. It can be built on fleeting trends rather than lasting talent or contribution. Think of the countless influencers who rise to prominence through a single viral post, only to fade into obscurity when the next trend emerges. This cycle of rapid ascent and descent raises important questions about the value of fame itself. Is it meaningful if it is so easily lost? Does it contribute to a sense of identity, or does it merely serve as a temporary distraction from the mundane?

The impact of these 15 minutes of fame extends beyond the individual. It shapes cultural conversations, influences trends, and can even impact societal values. When someone gains notoriety, their actions and words carry weight, often leading to broader discussions about the topics they represent. For instance, a viral moment can shine a spotlight on social issues, prompting dialogue and awareness. In this sense, the fleeting nature of fame can serve a purpose, pushing important conversations into the public arena.

However, there is also a darker side to this phenomenon. The intense scrutiny that comes with fame, even if brief, can be damaging. Individuals thrust into the limelight often face harsh criticism, invasive media coverage, and the loss of privacy. The psychological toll of fame, even for a short time, can lead to anxiety, depression, and a sense of isolation. The very thing that brings joy and recognition can also bring pain and distress.

In conclusion, 15 minutes of fame encapsulates a complex interplay of excitement, pressure, and societal reflection. It highlights the transient nature of recognition in a world that thrives on immediacy and novelty. While it can serve as a catalyst for change and awareness, it also poses significant challenges for those who find themselves in the spotlight. Ultimately, the question remains: is it worth it? In a culture that values fame, perhaps the real challenge lies not in seeking those fleeting moments but in finding meaning and purpose beyond the spotlight. Fame may be temporary, but the impact it leaves can echo far longer than just 15 minutes.

What Is A Money Shot?

The term "money shot" is often associated with the film industry, particularly within the realm of adult entertainment, but its usage has evolved and expanded across various fields, including photography, advertising, and even sports. To understand what constitutes a money shot, one must first recognize its fundamental definition: it is the shot or moment that is considered the most valuable or impactful, the one that draws the most attention and elicits the strongest response. In essence, it's the highlight, the pièce de résistance, the moment that can make or break a production, a campaign, or even a performance.

In adult films, the money shot typically refers to the climactic moment of sexual activity, often characterized by a specific visual or action that is deemed most appealing or provocative. This is the moment that is heavily promoted and anticipated, the reason viewers tune in. It encapsulates the essence of the film, representing not just the culmination of the narrative, but also the peak of sexual tension and release. The significance of this moment is paramount; it is often the most memorable part of the film, and its success can directly influence sales, ratings, and overall reception.

However, the concept of a money shot transcends the adult film industry. In mainstream cinema, for instance, a money shot might be a breathtaking visual effect, a gripping emotional moment, or a stunning piece of cinematography that leaves the audience in awe. Think of the iconic scenes in blockbuster films that are replayed in trailers and marketing materials. These moments are crafted to resonate with audiences, to evoke emotion, and to create buzz. They are the scenes that critics rave about, the ones that become part of cinematic lore.

In photography, the money shot is often the image that captures the essence of a subject or event. It's the photograph that tells a story, that conveys emotion, and that stands out among a myriad of other images. Photographers strive to capture that one moment that encapsulates the spirit of their subject, whether it's a candid shot of a child laughing, a breathtaking landscape at sunrise, or the raw emotion of a sports victory. This image is what can elevate a portfolio, draw attention to an exhibition, or even lead to viral fame in the age of social media.

In advertising, the money shot is the key visual or tagline that grabs the consumer's attention and compels them to engage with a product. It's the part of the ad that is designed to be memorable, to stick in the viewer's mind long after they've seen it. Advertisers meticulously craft these moments, often investing significant resources into ensuring that the money shot resonates with their target audience. This could be a stunning visual of a product in use, a clever play on words, or a celebrity endorsement that elevates the brand's status.

In sports, the money shot can refer to the game-winning moment, the play that defines a match, or the athlete's peak performance that is replayed in highlight reels. These moments are celebrated not just for their immediate impact but also for their long-lasting legacy. They become the defining moments of a career, the memories that fans cherish, and the narratives that sports commentators recount for years to come.

Ultimately, the money shot represents the pinnacle of impact, the moment that captures attention and evokes emotion across various domains. It is a testament to the power of visual storytelling, the art of capturing a fleeting moment that resonates deeply with an audience. Whether in film, photography, advertising, or sports, the money shot is a reminder of the importance of creating moments that matter, moments that linger in the mind long after they have passed. It's about distilling experiences into a single, powerful image or moment that encapsulates the essence of a narrative, leaving an indelible mark on the viewer.

What Is Post-Production?

Post production is a critical phase in the creation of any film, television show, or video project, serving as the bridge between the raw footage captured during production and the final product that audiences see. Often overlooked by those outside the industry, post production is a complex and multifaceted process that involves several key stages, each contributing to the overall quality and impact of the finished work. To understand what post production entails, it's essential to break it down into its primary components: editing, sound design, visual effects, color correction, and final delivery.

At its core, editing is the first step in post production. This is where the editor takes the raw footage shot during production and begins to assemble it into a coherent narrative. The editor sifts through hours of film, selecting the best takes, cutting out unnecessary scenes, and piecing together the story in a way that flows smoothly. This process involves not just technical skills but also a deep understanding of storytelling, pacing, and rhythm. The editor collaborates closely with the director to ensure that the vision for the project is realized, making creative decisions that can significantly alter the tone and emotional impact of the piece.

Once the editing is underway, sound design comes into play. Sound is a powerful tool in storytelling, and it can elevate a film from good to great. This stage involves the creation and manipulation of audio elements, including dialogue, sound effects, and background music. Sound designers work to enhance the auditory experience, ensuring that every sound complements the visuals on screen. Dialogue may need to be re-recorded in a process known as Automated Dialogue Replacement (ADR) to eliminate background noise or to improve clarity. Meanwhile, sound effects are added to create a more immersive environment, whether it's the rustling of leaves in a forest or the distant roar of a city. The final layer is the musical score, which can evoke emotions and underscore pivotal moments, guiding the audience's feelings throughout the film.

Visual effects (VFX) are another vital aspect of post production, particularly in projects that require elements beyond what can be captured on camera. This can range from subtle enhancements, like removing unwanted objects from a scene, to grand spectacles, such as creating entire worlds or creatures that do not exist in reality. VFX artists use a combination of software and artistic skill to create these elements, often working alongside the editor to seamlessly integrate them into the film. The goal is to make these effects as realistic as possible, so they enhance the story without drawing attention to themselves.

Color correction is also a crucial step in post production. This process involves adjusting the color and lighting of the footage to achieve a consistent look throughout the project. Colorists work to ensure that scenes match in tone, brightness, and saturation, creating a cohesive visual aesthetic. This can dramatically affect the mood of the film; for instance, cooler tones can evoke feelings of sadness or isolation, while warmer tones can create a sense of comfort or nostalgia. The color grading process is an art form in itself, often requiring a keen eye and a deep understanding of color theory.

Finally, the last step in post production is the final delivery of the project. This involves rendering the completed film into the appropriate format for distribution, whether it's for cinema, television, or streaming platforms. This stage also includes creating promotional materials, trailers, and other marketing content that will help to attract an audience.

In conclusion, post production is an intricate and essential part of the filmmaking process. It transforms raw footage into a polished, engaging final product through editing, sound design, visual effects, color correction, and delivery. Each of these elements plays a crucial role in shaping the audience's experience, making post production not just a technical necessity, but a vital creative endeavor that ultimately defines the success of a film or video project. Understanding post production allows us to appreciate the immense effort and artistry that goes into creating the stories we love to watch.

What Is A Key Grip?

The role of a key grip in the film industry is often misunderstood, overshadowed by the more glamorous titles like director or cinematographer. Yet, the key grip is an essential part of the filmmaking process, responsible for the physical aspects of lighting and camera movement. To understand the importance of a key grip, one must first appreciate the intricate dance that occurs on a film set, where every detail matters, and every crew member plays a vital role in bringing a vision to life.

At its core, the key grip is the head of the grip department, a team dedicated to manipulating lighting and camera equipment. Unlike the cinematographer, who focuses on the artistic and technical aspects of capturing images, the key grip is more of a hands-on technician. They work closely with the director of photography to ensure that the lighting is just right, adjusting flags, reflectors, and diffusers to create the desired effect. They are the ones who build and maintain the structures that hold lights, cameras, and other equipment, ensuring stability and safety on set.

The key grip's responsibilities extend beyond mere equipment management; they are also problem solvers. When a director envisions a complex shot, it is the key grip who figures out how to make it happen. Whether it's devising a way to rig a camera for a moving shot or creating a platform for a unique angle, the key grip uses their technical knowledge and creativity to overcome challenges. They must think on their feet, often making quick decisions to adapt to changing conditions, such as shifts in weather or last-minute adjustments to the shooting schedule.

One might wonder how one becomes a key grip. It typically starts with an understanding of the equipment used in film production. Many key grips begin their careers as grips, learning the ropes under the guidance of more experienced crew members. This hands-on experience is invaluable, as it allows aspiring grips to develop a deep knowledge of the tools of the trade, from C-stands to dollies, and to understand how each piece contributes to the overall production. Over time, through a combination of hard work, dedication, and networking, a grip may earn the trust and respect of their peers, paving the way to becoming a key grip.

Collaboration is at the heart of a key grip's role. They work closely with various departments, including lighting, camera, and production design. Communication is crucial; a key grip must be able to interpret the director's vision and translate it into practical applications. This often means being part of pre-production discussions, where they help plan the logistics of each scene. They may sketch out diagrams, discuss the best equipment to use, and even scout locations to determine how to approach each shot. This level of involvement ensures that when the cameras roll, everything is in place for a smooth shoot.

Moreover, the key grip plays a significant role in maintaining a safe environment on set. With heavy equipment and complex rigging, safety is paramount. The key grip is responsible for ensuring that all gear is secured and that the crew is aware of potential hazards. This duty requires a keen eye and a proactive approach to prevent accidents, safeguarding not only the crew but also the actors and the delicate equipment that brings a film to life.

In essence, a key grip is the unsung hero of the film set. They work tirelessly behind the scenes, often without recognition, yet their contributions are vital to the success of any production. Their expertise in equipment, problem-solving skills, and collaborative spirit ensure that the director's vision is realized, shot by shot. So, the next time you watch a film and marvel at its visuals, remember that there's a key grip somewhere behind the scenes, making it all possible, orchestrating the unseen elements that contribute to the magic of cinema.

What Is A Prequel?

A prequel is a narrative work that is set before the events of an existing story, often exploring the backstory of characters, settings, or events that have already been established. It serves to enrich the original narrative by providing context, depth, and a greater understanding of the motivations and histories of its characters. Think of it as a puzzle piece that fits into the larger picture, revealing details that might have been hinted at but never fully explored.

In literature, film, television, and even video games, prequels can take many forms, each uniquely contributing to the overarching narrative. They offer creators a chance to delve into the origins of beloved characters or to explore the events that led to a particular moment in the original work. This can be particularly compelling when the original story leaves questions unanswered or when the audience expresses a desire to know more about a character's past. For example, consider the prequels to popular film franchises. They often aim to capture the essence of what made the original work engaging while expanding the universe in which the characters exist.

One of the most notable aspects of prequels is their ability to play with audience expectations. When viewers or readers are already familiar with the outcomes of certain events, the tension shifts from uncertainty about what will happen next to a curiosity about how things came to be. This can create a unique kind of suspense, as audiences may find themselves on the edge of their seats, not because they fear for a character's life, but because they are eager to see how the pieces of the puzzle will come together.

Moreover, prequels can also serve as a means of character development. They provide an opportunity to showcase the growth or decline of a character, illustrating how past experiences shape present behaviors and decisions. For instance, a character who is perceived as a villain in the original story may be portrayed in a more sympathetic light in a prequel, allowing the audience to understand the circumstances that led to their darker choices. This recontextualization can challenge preconceived notions and invite viewers to engage with the character on a deeper level.

However, crafting a successful prequel is not without its challenges. It requires a delicate balance between honoring the original work and introducing new elements that feel fresh and engaging. If a prequel simply rehashes familiar events without adding significant depth, it risks disappointing fans who were eager for new insights. On the other hand, if it strays too far from the established narrative, it may alienate audiences who were drawn to the original story for specific reasons.

Additionally, the timeline of a prequel can complicate the storytelling process. Writers must be acutely aware of the events that have already taken place in the original work, ensuring that the prequel aligns with established lore and does not create contradictions. This requires meticulous planning and a deep understanding of the narrative universe, as even minor inconsistencies can disrupt the audience's immersion and undermine the credibility of the story.

In the realm of popular culture, we see numerous examples of successful prequels that have captivated audiences and enriched their respective franchises. Series like "Star Wars" and "Harry Potter" have expanded their universes through prequels, exploring the origins of iconic characters and pivotal events. These stories have not only satisfied fans' curiosity but have also introduced new generations to the rich tapestries of these beloved worlds.

Ultimately, a prequel serves as a bridge between the past and the present, allowing audiences to revisit familiar stories while simultaneously discovering new layers of meaning. It invites us to reflect on how history shapes identity and how the echoes of the past resonate in the present. In this way, prequels hold a unique place in storytelling, offering both nostalgia and innovation, and reminding us that every story is just one part of a much larger narrative.

What Is A Script Doctor?

A script doctor is a term that often floats around the film and television industry, yet many people remain unaware of what exactly it entails. At its core, a script doctor is a professional brought in to revise, rewrite, or polish a screenplay. Think of them as the secret weapon behind the scenes, the unsung heroes who take a script that might be floundering and breathe new life into it. Their role is not just about correcting typos or fixing grammatical errors; it's about enhancing the narrative, refining character arcs, and ensuring that the dialogue resonates with authenticity.

The need for script doctors arises from the complex nature of storytelling in visual media. A screenplay is not merely a blueprint for a film; it's a living document that evolves through various stages of production. Writers often face numerous challenges, whether it's a lack of clarity in the plot, underdeveloped characters, or pacing issues that disrupt the flow of the story. This is where a script doctor steps in. They analyze the script with a discerning eye, identifying weaknesses and areas for improvement. Their expertise lies in understanding what makes a story compelling and what audiences crave.

Script doctors come from diverse backgrounds. Some are seasoned screenwriters themselves, while others may have experience in directing, producing, or even acting. This variety equips them with a broad perspective on storytelling and the intricacies of character development. They possess a keen understanding of genre conventions, audience expectations, and industry trends. A good script doctor knows how to make a script not only better but also marketable, aligning it with current cinematic tastes without losing the original voice of the writer.

One common misconception is that script doctors take over a project entirely, overshadowing the original writer. In reality, the best script doctors work collaboratively, respecting the original vision while providing constructive feedback and suggestions. They might suggest a character's backstory be fleshed out, or perhaps recommend a plot twist that adds unexpected depth. The goal is to enhance the script, not to rewrite it from scratch. This collaborative process can lead to a richer, more engaging story that resonates with audiences and satisfies producers.

The process of script doctoring can vary widely. It may involve anything from a quick polish of dialogue to a complete overhaul of the narrative structure. Sometimes, a script doctor is brought in during the early stages of development, while other times, they might be called in during post-production when a film is struggling to find its footing. The timeline can be tight, and the pressure is immense, but that's where the skill of a script doctor shines. They thrive in high-stakes environments, often working under significant deadlines to deliver results that can make or break a project.

The compensation for script doctors can also be quite varied, often depending on their level of experience and the budget of the production. Some may work on a freelance basis, while others might be hired as part of a larger team. Regardless of the arrangement, a successful script doctor is often one whose contributions remain largely uncredited, operating in the shadows of the film industry while making a profound impact on the final product.

In an industry where the difference between a mediocre film and a blockbuster hit can come down to the strength of the script, the role of the script doctor cannot be understated. They are the ones who take the raw material of a screenplay and refine it, transforming it into a polished gem ready for the screen. Their work may go unnoticed by the general public, but for those in the know, a skilled script doctor is invaluable. They are the guardians of storytelling, ensuring that every script has the potential to captivate audiences and leave a lasting impression. So, the next time you watch a film that resonates deeply or a show that keeps you on the edge of your seat, remember that behind the scenes, there might just be a script doctor who played a crucial role in bringing that story to life.

What Is A Voice-Over?

Voice-over is a term that has permeated various facets of media, from film and television to advertising and video games. At its core, a voice-over is a production technique where a voice that is not part of the narrative is used in a variety of contexts to convey information, enhance storytelling, or provide commentary. This technique serves multiple purposes, and understanding its nuances can illuminate its significance in the world of media and communication.

To begin with, let's delve into the basic definition. A voice-over is typically recorded separately from the visual elements it accompanies. The voice can belong to a narrator, a character, or an unseen commentator, and it is generally used to provide insight, context, or emotional depth to the visuals. In film, for instance, a voice-over can help to articulate a character's inner thoughts, adding layers to their personality and motivations. This is often seen in films where a character reflects on past events or provides a personal commentary on the unfolding story.

In documentaries, voice-overs play a crucial role in guiding the audience through the narrative. They help to contextualize the visuals, providing background information, statistics, or expert opinions that enrich the viewer's understanding of the subject matter. The voice-over can transform a simple image into a powerful statement, providing clarity and depth that might be lost without it.

Furthermore, in the realm of advertising, voice-overs are a vital tool for persuasion. Advertisers utilize voice-overs to convey messages succinctly and effectively, often aiming to evoke emotions that resonate with potential customers. A well-crafted voice-over can create a connection between the product and the audience, influencing their perception and encouraging them to take action, whether that be purchasing a product, visiting a website, or engaging with a brand. The tone, pace, and inflection of the voice can significantly impact how the message is received, making the choice of voice talent critical in this context.

In the world of animation and video games, voice-overs bring characters to life, infusing them with personality and emotion. The voice actor's performance can make or break a character's appeal, transforming a static image into a relatable figure. This is especially true in video games, where players often form connections with characters through their voices, enhancing the overall gaming experience. The ability to convey emotion through voice alone is a remarkable skill, and voice actors play an essential role in crafting immersive narratives in these mediums.

Additionally, voice-overs are not limited to entertainment; they also extend to educational content, e-learning modules, and corporate training videos. Here, the voice-over serves to explain complex concepts, guide learners through processes, or provide instructions. The clarity of the voice and the pacing of the delivery are paramount in ensuring that the audience can absorb and understand the information being presented. This application of voice-over highlights its versatility in catering to different audiences and contexts.

In recent years, the rise of digital media and platforms has further expanded the scope of voice-over work. Podcasts, audiobooks, and online videos have created a demand for skilled voice-over artists who can engage listeners and convey information effectively. The growth of social media has also introduced new avenues for voice-over, with influencers and content creators utilizing voice to enhance their storytelling and connect with their audiences on a personal level.

In conclusion, a voice-over is a multifaceted tool that transcends mere narration. It is an art form that combines technical skill with emotional intelligence, capable of informing, entertaining, and persuading. Whether in a film, a commercial, a video game, or an educational video, the voice-over serves as a bridge between the creator's intent and the audience's experience. Its ability to convey meaning and emotion makes it an indispensable element of modern storytelling, enriching our engagement with the media we consume. Understanding what a voice-over is and its various applications deepens our appreciation for the craft and the voices that shape our narratives.

What Is An Opera?

Voice-over is a term that has permeated various facets of media, from film and television to advertising and video games. At its core, a voice-over is a production technique where a voice that is not part of the narrative is used in a variety of contexts to convey information, enhance storytelling, or provide commentary. This technique serves multiple purposes, and understanding its nuances can illuminate its significance in the world of media and communication.

To begin with, let's delve into the basic definition. A voice-over is typically recorded separately from the visual elements it accompanies. The voice can belong to a narrator, a character, or an unseen commentator, and it is generally used to provide insight, context, or emotional depth to the visuals. In film, for instance, a voice-over can help to articulate a character's inner thoughts, adding layers to their personality and motivations. This is often seen in films where a character reflects on past events or provides a personal commentary on the unfolding story.

In documentaries, voice-overs play a crucial role in guiding the audience through the narrative. They help to contextualize the visuals, providing background information, statistics, or expert opinions that enrich the viewer's understanding of the subject matter. The voice-over can transform a simple image into a powerful statement, providing clarity and depth that might be lost without it.

Furthermore, in the realm of advertising, voice-overs are a vital tool for persuasion. Advertisers utilize voice-overs to convey messages succinctly and effectively, often aiming to evoke emotions that resonate with potential customers. A well-crafted voice-over can create a connection between the product and the audience, influencing their perception and encouraging them to take action, whether that be purchasing a product, visiting a website, or engaging with a brand. The tone, pace, and inflection of the voice can significantly impact how the message is received, making the choice of voice talent critical in this context.

In the world of animation and video games, voice-overs bring characters to life, infusing them with personality and emotion. The voice actor's performance can make or break a character's appeal, transforming a static image into a relatable figure. This is especially true in video games, where players often form connections with characters through their voices, enhancing the overall gaming experience. The ability to convey emotion through voice alone is a remarkable skill, and voice actors play an essential role in crafting immersive narratives in these mediums.

Additionally, voice-overs are not limited to entertainment; they also extend to educational content, e-learning modules, and corporate training videos. Here, the voice-over serves to explain complex concepts, guide learners through processes, or provide instructions. The clarity of the voice and the pacing of the delivery are paramount in ensuring that the audience can absorb and understand the information being presented. This application of voice-over highlights its versatility in catering to different audiences and contexts.

In recent years, the rise of digital media and platforms has further expanded the scope of voice-over work. Podcasts, audiobooks, and online videos have created a demand for skilled voice-over artists who can engage listeners and convey information effectively. The growth of social media has also introduced new avenues for voice-over, with influencers and content creators utilizing voice to enhance their storytelling and connect with their audiences on a personal level.

In conclusion, a voice-over is a multifaceted tool that transcends mere narration. It is an art form that combines technical skill with emotional intelligence, capable of informing, entertaining, and persuading. Whether in a film, a commercial, a video game, or an educational video, the voice-over serves as a bridge between the creator's intent and the audience's experience. Its ability to convey meaning and emotion makes it an indispensable element of modern storytelling, enriching our engagement with the media we consume. Understanding what a voice-over is and its various applications deepens our appreciation for the craft and the voices that shape our narratives.

What Is A Black Comedy?

Black comedy, a genre often misunderstood, serves as a powerful lens through which we can examine the absurdity of life, death, and the human condition. At its core, black comedy intertwines humor with themes that are typically considered serious, taboo, or distressing. This unique blend challenges societal norms and invites audiences to confront uncomfortable truths through laughter. It's a delicate balancing act, walking the tightrope between comedy and tragedy, where the punchline often emerges from the darkest corners of existence.

The roots of black comedy can be traced back to ancient literature and theater, where playwrights and authors explored themes of mortality, suffering, and the grotesque. Think of Shakespeare's "Hamlet," which, despite its heavy themes, is peppered with moments of wit and irony. The character of the grave digger, for instance, offers a comedic respite amidst the play's exploration of death and madness. This interplay between humor and despair has evolved over centuries, finding its way into modern cinema, literature, and stand-up comedy.

In contemporary culture, black comedy often manifests in films and television shows that tackle subjects like illness, crime, and societal dysfunction. Consider the cult classic "Dr. Strangelove," which satirizes the absurdity of nuclear war. The film's comedic portrayal of serious geopolitical tensions serves as a critique of the very real fears of the Cold War era. Similarly, shows like "The Office" or "It's Always Sunny in Philadelphia" use humor to explore the mundane yet often bleak realities of everyday life, highlighting the absurdity of human behavior in the face of adversity.

One of the defining characteristics of black comedy is its ability to provoke thought while eliciting laughter. It invites audiences to reflect on the complexities of human experience, often forcing them to grapple with their own discomfort. This genre challenges the notion that humor must always be light-hearted or uplifting. Instead, it posits that laughter can emerge from the darkest places, offering a form of catharsis. By confronting the unsettling aspects of life, black comedy provides a safe space for audiences to explore their fears and anxieties.

However, black comedy is not without its controversies. The line between humor and insensitivity can be razor-thin, and what one person finds hilarious, another may deem offensive. This dichotomy raises important questions about the ethics of comedy and the responsibility of creators. In a world where social issues are increasingly at the forefront, the challenge lies in navigating these sensitive topics with care while still delivering impactful humor. Successful black comedies often rely on a nuanced understanding of their subject matter, ensuring that the humor does not trivialize the pain or suffering of others.

Moreover, black comedy can serve as a form of social commentary, critiquing societal norms and injustices. By using humor to address difficult subjects, creators can shed light on issues that might otherwise be overlooked. For instance, films like "Get Out" and "Jojo Rabbit" tackle racism and prejudice through the lens of black comedy, prompting audiences to reflect on their own beliefs and biases. This genre can be a powerful tool for change, using laughter to foster dialogue and promote understanding.

In essence, black comedy is a celebration of the absurdity of life. It acknowledges the darkness that exists within the human experience while simultaneously finding ways to laugh at it. By embracing the uncomfortable and the taboo, black comedy encourages us to confront our fears, question societal norms, and ultimately, find solace in the shared experience of being human. It reminds us that even in our darkest moments, humor can be a source of connection, resilience, and understanding. So, the next time you find yourself chuckling at a film or a joke that delves into the macabre, remember: you're not just laughing; you're engaging with the complexities of life itself.

What Is A Cold Open?

A cold open, also known as a teaser, is a narrative device commonly used in television shows, films, and even some forms of literature. It refers to the practice of starting a program or a scene without any prior introduction or credits, immediately plunging the audience into the action or a compelling moment. This technique serves several purposes, primarily aimed at grabbing the viewer's attention right from the outset. The term itself is derived from the idea of beginning "cold," without any warm-up or gradual buildup. It's a way to engage the audience immediately, creating intrigue and drawing them into the story without delay.

Historically, cold opens have been used in various forms of media, but they gained significant popularity in television during the 1970s and 1980s. Shows like "Saturday Night Live" and "The Office" have become well-known for their effective use of cold opens, often delivering punchy jokes or dramatic moments that set the tone for the episode. The effectiveness of a cold open lies in its ability to establish the mood, introduce key themes, or present critical plot points without the need for lengthy exposition. Instead of a slow build-up, viewers are immediately confronted with something that piques their interest, whether it's a humorous skit, a shocking event, or a pivotal character moment.

This technique can also serve to establish character dynamics or relationships quickly. For instance, in a sitcom, a cold open might showcase a humorous interaction between two characters that encapsulates their relationship, setting the stage for the episode's unfolding narrative. In more dramatic series, a cold open might present a cliffhanger or a moment of tension that hooks the audience, compelling them to continue watching to see how the situation resolves. It's a strategic approach that recognizes the decreasing attention spans of modern audiences, who often decide within seconds whether to continue watching a program.

Moreover, cold opens can serve as a narrative device that allows for creative storytelling. They can be standalone scenes that don't necessarily tie into the main storyline, providing a moment of levity or a flash of insight into a character's life. In some cases, they are designed to mislead the audience, presenting a scenario that seems significant but ultimately serves as a red herring, leading to a twist later in the episode. This element of surprise can enhance viewer engagement, as audiences become invested in the unfolding narrative, eager to see how the initial moment connects to the larger story.

In terms of structure, a cold open typically lasts anywhere from a few seconds to several minutes, depending on the format of the show. In half-hour sitcoms, it might be a quick, punchy scene that lasts around a minute or two. In hour-long dramas, the cold open can be more elaborate, setting up complex scenarios that require more time to establish. Regardless of the length, the key is to create a moment that resonates with the audience, making them want to stick around for the rest of the episode.

In conclusion, a cold open is a powerful storytelling tool that serves to engage the audience right from the start. It's a technique that has evolved over the years, becoming a staple in modern television and film. By bypassing traditional introductions and plunging directly into the action, cold opens create an immediate connection with viewers, drawing them into the narrative and setting the tone for what's to come. Whether through humor, drama, or intrigue, the effectiveness of a cold open lies in its ability to captivate and maintain audience interest, reminding us that sometimes, the best way to start is simply to dive in.

What Is the Difference between Latino, Chicano, and Hispanic?

When we talk about identity in the context of culture and ethnicity, the terms Latino, Chicano, and Hispanic often come up, and while they may seem interchangeable at first glance, they each carry distinct meanings and histories that are important to understand. Let's start with the term Hispanic. This word generally refers to people from Spanish-speaking countries, which includes Spain and most of Latin America, as well as those who share a cultural connection to the Spanish language. The term gained popularity in the United States during the 1970s as a way to categorize a diverse group of people under one label for demographic purposes. However, it is crucial to note that not everyone who speaks Spanish identifies as Hispanic. For instance, many individuals from Brazil, where Portuguese is the official language, do not fit into this category despite being part of Latin America. Additionally, the term can feel limiting, as it focuses primarily on language rather than the rich tapestry of cultural identities that exist among Spanish-speaking populations.

Now, let's move on to Latino. This term is broader than Hispanic and refers specifically to people from Latin America, regardless of their language. It encompasses a wide range of cultures, ethnicities, and histories. Latino includes individuals from countries like Mexico, Puerto Rico, Cuba, the Dominican Republic, and many others in Central and South America. It is a gender-neutral term, while its feminine counterpart, Latina, is often used to refer to women. The use of Latino has gained traction as a way to emphasize a shared geographical and cultural heritage rather than just a linguistic one. However, even Latino can be seen as a somewhat homogenizing label, as it does not account for the diverse Indigenous, Afro-Latino, and other cultural influences that exist within these communities.

Now, let's delve into Chicano. This term is more specific and carries a historical and political significance that sets it apart from the other two. Chicano is primarily used to describe people of Mexican descent who are born or live in the United States. The term emerged during the Chicano civil rights movement in the 1960s and 1970s, which sought to address issues of social justice, discrimination, and cultural pride among Mexican Americans. Chicano identity is deeply intertwined with the struggle for recognition and rights, and it often reflects a sense of pride in one's Mexican heritage while also embracing the complexities of being Mexican American. Unlike Hispanic and Latino, which can sometimes be used in a more general sense, Chicano is a term that resonates with a specific political and cultural context. It embodies a reclaiming of identity and a rejection of assimilation into mainstream American culture.

In conversations about identity, it's essential to recognize that these terms are not just labels; they represent lived experiences and histories. People may choose to identify with one term over another based on personal preference, cultural background, or political beliefs. For instance, some individuals may prefer to identify as Chicano to honor their political heritage, while others may feel more comfortable with Latino or Hispanic due to their broader cultural connections.

Moreover, the conversation around these identities is continually evolving. New terms and identities are emerging as people seek to express their multifaceted experiences in a world that is increasingly interconnected yet still grapples with issues of race, ethnicity, and belonging.

Ultimately, understanding the differences between Latino, Chicano, and Hispanic is not just an academic exercise; it is a way to honor the diverse narratives that contribute to the rich mosaic of culture and identity in the United States and beyond. When we engage with these terms thoughtfully, we can foster a deeper appreciation for the complexities of identity and the stories that shape who we are as individuals and communities.

What Does It Mean To "Take A Chill Pill"?

Taking a chill pill is an expression that has permeated our culture, often used in casual conversation to suggest that someone should relax or calm down. But what does it truly mean to take a chill pill? At its core, this phrase encapsulates a broader idea about managing stress and anxiety in our fast-paced world. It speaks to the necessity of finding balance in our lives, particularly in an era where pressures—both personal and societal—are omnipresent.

To understand this expression, we first need to delve into the concept of stress itself. Stress is a natural response to challenges or demands, but chronic stress can lead to a myriad of health issues, both mental and physical. When someone tells you to take a chill pill, they're essentially encouraging you to step back from whatever is causing you distress and to take a moment for yourself. It's a reminder that life is not just about deadlines and responsibilities; it's also about finding moments of peace and tranquility amidst the chaos.

Now, let's unpack the metaphor of a "chill pill." While it may sound like a whimsical reference to a magical remedy, it implies a more profound truth: that we often need to take deliberate actions to calm our minds and bodies. The idea of a pill suggests a quick fix, something that can be swallowed to alleviate discomfort. However, in reality, taking a chill pill is often about developing habits and practices that promote relaxation and mental clarity. It could mean engaging in mindfulness meditation, practicing yoga, or simply taking a few deep breaths to center oneself.

The act of taking a chill pill is also about recognizing the importance of self-care. In a world that constantly demands our attention, we often forget to prioritize our own well-being. We become so enmeshed in our responsibilities—work, family, social obligations—that we neglect to check in with ourselves. Taking a chill pill is an invitation to pause, to reflect, and to recharge. It encourages us to set boundaries, to say no when necessary, and to allocate time for activities that bring us joy and relaxation.

Moreover, the phrase embodies the concept of emotional regulation. In moments of anger, frustration, or anxiety, it can be easy to react impulsively. But taking a chill pill is about stepping back from those immediate emotions and assessing the situation with a clearer mind. It's a call to cultivate patience and understanding, both for ourselves and for others. When we take a moment to chill, we gain perspective, and that perspective can lead to healthier interactions and decisions.

However, it's essential to recognize that taking a chill pill doesn't imply ignoring problems or avoiding responsibilities. It's not about escapism; rather, it's about equipping ourselves with the tools to face challenges head-on. By taking time to decompress, we can approach our tasks with renewed energy and focus. This proactive approach to stress management can enhance our productivity and creativity, allowing us to tackle our responsibilities with a clear mind and a light heart.

In essence, taking a chill pill is a metaphor for embracing a lifestyle that prioritizes mental health and well-being. It's a reminder that we are not just human doings, but human beings, deserving of rest and relaxation. In a society that often glorifies busyness, taking a chill pill is a radical act of self-love. It's a declaration that we are worthy of peace, that we can step away from the noise, and that we can find solace within ourselves.

So, the next time someone suggests you take a chill pill, consider it a gentle nudge towards self-care and mindfulness. Embrace the idea that it's okay to slow down, to breathe, and to find your center. Because in doing so, you're not just taking a chill pill; you're choosing to live a more balanced, fulfilling life.

What Is A 12-Bar Blues Progression?

The 12-bar blues progression is a musical structure that serves as the backbone of countless blues songs and has influenced a multitude of genres, including rock, jazz, and even pop. At its core, the 12-bar blues is a simple yet profound framework that allows for both emotional expression and improvisational freedom. It consists of just three chords, typically the I, IV, and V chords of a given key. To break it down further, let's take the key of C as an example. In this case, the I chord would be C, the IV chord would be F, and the V chord would be G.

The structure unfolds over twelve measures, or bars, which is where the term "12-bar" comes from. The first four bars typically feature the I chord, establishing the tonal center. This is where the listener gets a sense of home, a foundation that feels familiar and comforting. The next two bars introduce the IV chord, creating a sense of tension or movement away from that home base. It's like stepping out of your front door and into the world, feeling the excitement of the unknown while still tethered to the familiarity of your own space.

Then, the progression returns to the I chord for another two bars, reaffirming that sense of home before venturing into the V chord for one bar. This moment is crucial; it's the point where the tension peaks, and the anticipation builds. It's as if you're standing at the edge of a cliff, ready to leap into the unknown. Finally, the progression resolves with the IV chord for one bar, followed by a return to the I chord for the last two bars, bringing everything back full circle. This cyclical nature of the

12-bar blues creates a satisfying sense of closure, making it a powerful tool for songwriters and performers alike.

Historically, the 12-bar blues has its roots in African American musical traditions, with origins tracing back to the late 19th and early 20th centuries. It emerged from the work songs, spirituals, and folk music of African Americans in the southern United States. The emotional depth of the blues often reflects the struggles and hardships faced by these communities, making it not just a musical form but a vehicle for storytelling and expression. As the genre evolved, it found its way into the mainstream, influencing artists across various musical landscapes.

One of the most remarkable aspects of the 12-bar blues progression is its versatility. While the basic structure remains the same, musicians can infuse their own styles and interpretations. They might add seventh chords, which introduce a slightly dissonant sound that enhances the emotional weight of the music. They might also incorporate variations, such as quick changes, where the IV chord is introduced earlier in the progression, or even shifts in rhythm that create a more complex feel.

Improvisation is another key element of the 12-bar blues. Musicians often use the chord changes as a canvas, painting their own melodies and solos over the established framework. This improvisational aspect allows for individual expression, making each performance unique. It's a conversation between the musicians, a dynamic interplay where ideas are exchanged, and creativity flourishes.

In contemporary music, the influence of the 12-bar blues is undeniable. It can be heard in the works of legendary artists like B.B. King, Muddy Waters, and Eric Clapton, as well as in modern rock and pop songs. Its simplicity and emotional resonance continue to captivate audiences, proving that sometimes, the most profound expressions come from the simplest of structures.

So, whether you're a musician looking to dive into the rich world of blues or simply someone curious about the roots of modern music, understanding the 12-bar blues progression offers a glimpse into a timeless tradition that celebrates the human experience through sound. It's a reminder that in music, as in life, we often return to familiar places, finding new meanings and stories with each journey.

What Is A Sleeper Cell?

A sleeper cell is a term that evokes images of hidden dangers and covert operations, yet its meaning is often shrouded in misunderstanding. At its core, a sleeper cell refers to a group of individuals who are part of a larger organization, typically a terrorist group, but remain inactive or dormant until they receive orders to act. These individuals blend into society, often living seemingly normal lives, while maintaining allegiance to their cause. The concept of a sleeper cell raises significant questions about loyalty, deception, and the very nature of security in a world where threats can lurk in plain sight.

The origins of sleeper cells can be traced back to various historical contexts, but they gained prominence in the late 20th century, particularly in relation to international terrorism. Groups such as Al-Qaeda and ISIS have utilized sleeper cells as a strategic method to carry out attacks in various countries. The advantage of a sleeper cell lies in its ability to operate under the radar, allowing members to gather intelligence, build networks, and prepare for operations without drawing attention to themselves. This method of operation complicates the work of law enforcement and intelligence agencies, as the threat is not always visible until it is too late.

The recruitment of individuals into sleeper cells often involves a complex process of radicalization. This can occur through various means, including social media, personal connections, or even in religious institutions. Once individuals are recruited, they are trained to adopt a dual identity—one that fits seamlessly into their everyday life and another that aligns with the extremist ideology they have embraced. This duality is crucial; it allows them to evade detection while remaining loyal to their cause. The psychological aspect of this recruitment process is fascinating, as it taps into fundamental human needs such as belonging, purpose, and identity.

The operational structure of sleeper cells varies, but they often consist of small, tightly knit groups. This minimizes the risk of exposure, as members are less likely to betray one another. Communication is typically conducted through secure channels, and operational plans are kept vague to prevent leaks. When the time comes to act, these cells can mobilize quickly and efficiently, leveraging their knowledge of the local environment to execute their plans. The attacks can range from bombings to shootings, each designed to instill fear and chaos while advancing the agenda of the group.

The existence of sleeper cells poses significant challenges for national security. Intelligence agencies must constantly be on high alert, employing a variety of methods to detect and dismantle these cells before they can carry out their plans. This includes monitoring communications, conducting surveillance, and infiltrating potential networks. However, the balance between security and civil liberties becomes a contentious issue. The fear of sleeper cells can lead to increased scrutiny of certain communities, often resulting in racial profiling and stigmatization. This creates a paradox where the very measures taken to ensure safety can inadvertently foster division and mistrust within society.

Public awareness of sleeper cells is crucial in the fight against terrorism. Understanding the signs of radicalization and the methods used by these groups can empower communities to take action. Education plays a vital role in countering extremist narratives and providing individuals with the tools to resist recruitment efforts. Furthermore, fostering open dialogue between communities and law enforcement can help build trust and cooperation, making it more difficult for sleeper cells to operate undetected.

In conclusion, a sleeper cell is not merely a group of individuals waiting in the shadows; it embodies the complexities of modern threats to security. It challenges our understanding of loyalty, identity, and the lengths to which individuals will go for their beliefs. As society grapples with the realities of terrorism, recognizing the existence and implications of sleeper cells is essential in creating a safer, more informed world. The battle against these hidden threats is ongoing, requiring vigilance, understanding, and a commitment to addressing the root causes of extremism.

What Is A Swiss Army Knife?

The Swiss Army Knife, a marvel of engineering and design, is more than just a tool; it embodies versatility, practicality, and a spirit of adventure. Originating in Switzerland in the late 19th century, this multi-functional instrument was initially created for the Swiss Army to assist soldiers in a variety of tasks. The concept was simple yet revolutionary: combine multiple tools into a single, compact device that could be easily carried. The first model, produced in 1891, featured a blade, a can opener, and a screwdriver. It was a modest beginning, but it laid the groundwork for what would become an iconic symbol of ingenuity.

As the years progressed, the Swiss Army Knife evolved, incorporating more tools and features to meet the needs of its users. Today, you can find models equipped with a staggering array of implements, including scissors, pliers, wire cutters, saws, and even specialized tools like fish scalers and corkscrews. The sheer variety is astounding, with some knives boasting over thirty functions, making them suitable for everything from camping trips to everyday tasks around the house. This adaptability is one of the key reasons the Swiss Army Knife has gained a reputation as the ultimate multi-tool.

The construction of a Swiss Army Knife is a testament to Swiss craftsmanship. Each knife is meticulously designed and manufactured with precision. The materials used, typically high-quality stainless steel for the blades and durable polymers for the handle, ensure longevity and reliability. The iconic red handle, often adorned with the Swiss cross, is instantly recognizable and has become synonymous with quality and functionality. This attention to detail is not just about aesthetics; it reflects a commitment to performance and durability that users have come to expect.

Beyond its physical attributes, the Swiss Army Knife holds a special place in popular culture. It has been featured in countless movies, books, and television shows, often symbolizing resourcefulness and preparedness. The phrase "Swiss Army Knife" has even transcended its literal meaning, coming to represent any tool or solution that is versatile enough to handle a variety of situations. This cultural significance adds to its allure, making it not just a practical item, but a beloved icon.

The utility of the Swiss Army Knife is perhaps best illustrated through anecdotes of those who have relied on it in times of need. Hikers have used it to slice through rope, open cans of food, and even perform minor repairs on their gear. Campers have relied on it to start fires, prepare meals, and tackle unexpected challenges in the wilderness. It has been a companion on countless adventures, providing peace of mind that one is prepared for whatever may arise. This reliability fosters a sense of confidence and independence, allowing users to embrace life's uncertainties with a trusty tool at their side.

Moreover, the Swiss Army Knife is not just for outdoor enthusiasts. It has found its place in urban environments, serving as a handy tool for everyday tasks. From opening packages to making quick repairs, its functionality extends far beyond the realms of camping and survival. In a world where convenience is paramount, the Swiss Army Knife stands out as a solution that combines practicality with portability.

In conclusion, the Swiss Army Knife is a remarkable tool that transcends its simple design. It represents the pinnacle of versatility and functionality, embodying the spirit of innovation that has become synonymous with Swiss craftsmanship. Whether in the hands of a soldier, a camper, or an everyday user, it serves as a reminder that sometimes, the simplest solutions can be the most effective. This little red knife has carved out a significant place in history, culture, and the hearts of those who appreciate its unwavering reliability and boundless potential. It is not merely a tool; it is a symbol of preparedness, creativity, and the adventurous spirit that resides in us all.

What Is A Shuriken?

A shuriken is often misrepresented in popular culture as a mere ninja throwing star, a weapon of stealth and surprise that flings through the air with deadly precision. While it is indeed a tool used in the martial arts arsenal of the ninjas, the reality of the shuriken is far more complex and rich in history. The term "shuriken" itself translates to "hidden hand blade," which gives us insight into its purpose: it was designed to be a concealed weapon, utilized not just for direct confrontation but also as a means of distraction or diversion. This multifaceted nature of the shuriken is what makes it an intriguing subject of study.

Historically, shuriken originated in Japan, with roots tracing back to the feudal periods of the country. They were created by the samurai and later adopted by the ninja, who honed their skills in espionage and guerrilla warfare. The earliest forms of shuriken were not the star-shaped objects that we often envision today. Instead, they came in various shapes and sizes, including pointed spikes or flat, disc-like forms. These variations were crafted from materials like metal, wood, or even stone, depending on the resources available and the intended use.

The purpose of a shuriken was not solely to injure or kill. In many cases, they were used to create a distraction. Imagine a ninja slipping through the shadows, throwing a shuriken into the distance to draw the attention of guards away from their true objective. This tactic allowed for stealthy movements and successful infiltration. The shuriken was also employed to disarm or incapacitate an opponent briefly, providing the user with an advantage in combat.

The design of shuriken can be quite intricate. The most recognizable form is the four-pointed star, but there are also types like the bo-shuriken, which is a long, pointed spike, and the hira-shuriken, which resembles a flat disc. Each type has its own method of throwing and intended purpose. For example, the bo-shuriken is often thrown with a flicking motion of the wrist, while the hira-shuriken is typically thrown in a spinning motion, allowing for greater distance and accuracy.

In addition to their physical attributes, shuriken also carry symbolic weight. They represent the cunning and resourcefulness of the ninja, embodying the idea that victory does not always come from brute strength but rather from intelligence and strategy. The shuriken is a testament to the philosophy that sometimes, the most effective approach is to remain unseen, to strike from the shadows, and to use one's environment to gain the upper hand.

The cultural significance of shuriken extends beyond their practical use in combat. They have become iconic symbols in various forms of media, from films and video games to anime and manga. This portrayal, while often exaggerated and romanticized, has contributed to the enduring fascination with ninjas and their tools. Yet, it is essential to recognize that the shuriken is not just a fictional trope; it is a historical artifact that provides insight into the martial practices of ancient Japan.

In modern times, shuriken have found a place in martial arts training and competitions, where practitioners learn to throw them with precision and skill. They also appear in historical reenactments and demonstrations, allowing contemporary audiences to appreciate the craftsmanship and tactical significance of these unique weapons.

In conclusion, a shuriken is much more than a simple throwing star; it is a complex tool rooted in history, strategy, and cultural significance. Its design, purpose, and the philosophy it represents offer a glimpse into the world of the ninja, where skill, cunning, and the element of surprise were paramount. Understanding the shuriken in its entirety allows us to appreciate not just its role in combat but also its place in the rich tapestry of Japanese history and culture.

What Is A Pop-Up Tent?

A pop-up tent is a type of portable shelter designed for ease of use and convenience, primarily favored by campers, festival-goers, and outdoor enthusiasts. Unlike traditional tents that require time-consuming assembly, a pop-up tent can be set up in mere seconds, making it an attractive option for those who value simplicity and efficiency. The mechanism behind this rapid setup lies in a flexible frame that is pre-attached to the fabric of the tent. When removed from its carrying bag, the tent springs into shape, allowing users to secure it with minimal effort. This makes it an ideal choice for spontaneous outings or situations where time is of the essence.

The design of pop-up tents typically features a dome shape, which not only contributes to their aesthetic appeal but also enhances their stability against wind and rain. Most models are constructed from lightweight materials, such as polyester or nylon, and often include waterproof coatings to keep the interior dry. The floor is usually made from a durable material that can withstand rough terrain, ensuring that users are protected from moisture and dirt. Many pop-up tents also come equipped with mesh windows and vents, allowing for ventilation while keeping insects at bay. This combination of features makes them suitable for a variety of outdoor settings, from beaches to music festivals and camping trips.

One of the primary advantages of pop-up tents is their portability. They are typically lightweight and compact when folded, making them easy to carry in a backpack or in the trunk of a car. This portability is particularly beneficial for those who enjoy hiking or traveling to remote locations where carrying heavy gear would be impractical. Additionally, many pop-up tents come with a carrying case, further enhancing their ease of transport. This convenience encourages more people to engage in outdoor activities, as the hassle of setting up a traditional tent can often be a deterrent.

However, while pop-up tents excel in quick setup and portability, they may not always provide the same level of durability and weather resistance as more robust camping tents. Their lightweight materials can be susceptible to wear and tear, particularly with frequent use or exposure to harsh conditions. For this reason, it is important for users to consider the environment in which they plan to use the tent. For casual outings or short trips in mild weather, a pop-up tent can be an excellent choice. However, for extended camping trips in unpredictable climates, a more traditional tent may be advisable.

Another aspect to consider is the size and capacity of pop-up tents. They come in various sizes, accommodating anywhere from one to several people. Some models are designed specifically for solo campers, while others can fit families or groups. When selecting a pop-up tent, it is crucial to assess the number of occupants and the amount of gear that needs to be stored inside. Many pop-up tents also feature additional storage options, such as pockets or hooks for hanging items, which can be useful for keeping the interior organized.

In conclusion, a pop-up tent is a versatile and user-friendly option for those seeking a portable shelter for outdoor activities. Its rapid setup, lightweight design, and compactness make it particularly appealing for spontaneous adventures. While it may not offer the same level of durability as traditional tents, it serves as an excellent option for casual outings in favorable weather conditions. When choosing a pop-up tent, one must consider factors such as size, material, and intended use to ensure it meets their specific needs. With the right pop-up tent in hand, outdoor enthusiasts can enjoy the beauty of nature with minimal hassle, allowing for more time spent making memories rather than wrestling with complicated gear.

What Is A Victimless Crime?

A victimless crime is often defined as an act that is prohibited by law but does not directly harm or violate the rights of another individual. It raises intriguing questions about morality, legality, and the very nature of crime itself. At its core, the concept challenges the traditional understanding of crime, which typically involves a clear victim suffering harm or loss due to the actions of another. Yet, in the realm of victimless crimes, the narrative shifts dramatically. Instead of a straightforward perpetrator and victim dynamic, we find ourselves navigating a complex landscape of personal choice, societal norms, and the role of government in regulating behavior.

Consider, for example, drug use. Many argue that when an individual chooses to use drugs, they are only harming themselves, thus making it a victimless crime. Yet, the implications of drug use often extend beyond the individual. Families may suffer, communities may experience increased crime rates, and public health systems may become overburdened as a result of addiction. This raises the question: can a crime truly be victimless if the consequences ripple outwards, affecting others in the community? The debate becomes even more intricate when we consider the varying perspectives on what constitutes harm. Some view drug use as a personal liberty, a choice that should be respected, while others see it as a societal ill that requires regulation and intervention.

Another quintessential example of a victimless crime is prostitution. In many jurisdictions, engaging in sex work is illegal, yet those who participate often argue that they are consenting adults making choices about their own bodies and lives. Advocates for decriminalization assert that the criminalization of prostitution does more harm than good, pushing sex workers into dangerous situations and denying them legal protections. Critics, however, argue that prostitution can lead to exploitation and trafficking, suggesting that there are victims within this transaction, even if they are not immediately visible. This dichotomy illustrates the tension between individual autonomy and societal responsibility, a central theme in discussions about victimless crimes.

Then we have gambling, another area often labeled as a victimless crime. Many people gamble responsibly, enjoying it as a form of entertainment without adverse effects. Yet, for others, gambling can spiral into addiction, leading to financial ruin and strained relationships. The question arises: should the government intervene to protect individuals from their own choices, or is it a matter of personal responsibility? The legalization of gambling in many places has sparked debates about regulation, morality, and the extent to which the state should involve itself in the private lives of citizens.

The concept of victimless crimes also intersects with issues of morality and ethics. Laws are often reflections of societal values, and what one culture may deem acceptable, another may not. For instance, the legality of same-sex relationships and marriage has evolved significantly over time, with many previously viewing it as a moral failing or a crime against societal norms. The shift towards acceptance highlights how societal perceptions of victimless crimes can change, often driven by a growing understanding of human rights and personal freedom.

As we delve deeper into this topic, it becomes clear that the label of "victimless" is not as simple as it appears. It invites us to examine the broader implications of our laws and the societal structures that uphold them. It forces us to confront uncomfortable truths about personal choice, societal impact, and the role of government in our lives. In a world where the lines between right and wrong are often blurred, the discussion of victimless crimes serves as a reminder that the consequences of our actions, whether direct or indirect, can ripple through the fabric of society in ways we may not fully comprehend. Ultimately, the exploration of victimless crimes challenges us to reflect on our values, our responsibilities to one another, and the intricate web of choices that define our collective existence.

What do People Mean By An "800 Pound Gorilla"?

When people refer to an "800-pound gorilla," they are invoking a metaphor that has become a part of everyday language, often used to describe a situation or entity that holds significant power or dominance, yet may not always be acknowledged or addressed. The phrase itself originates from the idea that if there were an 800-pound gorilla in the room, it would be impossible to ignore. It symbolizes an overwhelming presence, one that commands attention and influences the dynamics of any situation. This metaphor can be applied across various contexts, from business and politics to social issues and personal relationships.

In a business context, the 800-pound gorilla often represents a major player in an industry—think of a large corporation that has the resources, market share, and influence to shape trends and practices. This company, due to its vast size and capabilities, can dictate terms, set prices, and often overshadow smaller competitors. For instance, when we look at the technology sector, companies like Apple or Google can be seen as the 800-pound gorillas. Their innovations and market strategies can shift the entire landscape, leaving smaller firms scrambling to keep up. The presence of such a dominant player can create a challenging environment for competition, as these companies can leverage their power to influence regulations, consumer behavior, and even the direction of technological advancement.

In politics, the term takes on a slightly different nuance but retains its core meaning. An 800-pound gorilla in this realm might refer to a powerful lobby, a dominant political party, or even a charismatic leader who can sway public opinion and policy decisions. For example, in the United States, we often see how certain interest groups—such as those representing the pharmaceutical industry or the National Rifle Association—act as the 800-pound gorillas of political discourse. Their financial clout and organizational strength enable them to exert considerable influence over lawmakers and the legislative process, often overshadowing the voices of average citizens. This dynamic can lead to a sense of frustration among the public, as these powerful entities can sideline pressing issues that may not align with their interests.

Socially, the metaphor can highlight issues that are significant yet often overlooked. It could refer to systemic problems like climate change or social inequality—issues that loom large and demand attention but are frequently ignored in favor of more immediate concerns. When we consider climate change, for instance, the scientific consensus is clear: we are facing a crisis of monumental proportions. Yet, discussions around it can be sidelined by short-term economic interests or political posturing. In this sense, the 800-pound gorilla represents the urgent need for action against formidable challenges that may not be adequately addressed in public discourse.

Additionally, on a personal level, the term can refer to dynamics within relationships or groups. An individual might find themselves in a situation where a dominant personality—perhaps a family member or a close friend—holds sway over decisions and discussions, creating an imbalance that can lead to resentment or conflict. Recognizing this "gorilla" can be the first step toward addressing underlying tensions and fostering healthier communication.

Ultimately, the phrase "800-pound gorilla" serves as a powerful reminder of the forces that shape our lives, whether they are economic, political, social, or personal. It urges us to confront these dominant entities and issues rather than ignore them, acknowledging their presence and influence. In doing so, we can begin to navigate the complexities they introduce, seeking balance and fairness in our interactions and decisions. By understanding what the 800-pound gorilla represents, we gain insight into the structures of power that govern our world, empowering us to challenge the status quo and advocate for change where it is needed most.

What Is The Difference Between Distilled, Purified, Mineral, Well, And Spring Water?

Water is essential to life, yet not all water is created equal. When we stroll through the grocery store, we often see a myriad of bottled water options, each boasting its unique benefits and properties. But what really distinguishes distilled, purified, mineral, well, and spring water from one another? Understanding these differences can help us make informed choices about what we consume.

Let's start with distilled water. Distillation is a process that involves boiling water to create steam, then cooling that steam to form liquid water again. This method effectively removes impurities, minerals, and contaminants, resulting in water that is nearly pure H2O. Distilled water is often used in laboratories and medical settings, where the absence of minerals is crucial. However, because it lacks minerals, some people find it flat or tasteless. It's important to note that while distilled water is free from impurities, it may not provide the essential minerals our bodies need, which is why it's not the most popular choice for everyday hydration.

Next, we have purified water. Purification can be achieved through various methods, including reverse osmosis, filtration, or distillation. The goal is to remove contaminants and impurities, resulting in water that meets or exceeds the standards set by the Environmental Protection Agency. Purified water can come from any source, including tap water, and is often treated to ensure it's safe for drinking. This type of water is popular for its clean taste and safety, making it a common choice for those looking to avoid the potential impurities found in untreated water.

Now, let's explore mineral water. This type of water is sourced from natural springs and contains a significant amount of dissolved minerals, such as calcium, magnesium, and potassium. These minerals can contribute to the taste and health benefits of the water. Mineral water is often touted for its potential health benefits, including aiding digestion and providing essential nutrients. However, it's important to note that the mineral content can vary widely depending on the source. Some brands even add minerals back into the water after treatment to enhance flavor and nutritional value. For those seeking a refreshing beverage that offers more than just hydration, mineral water can be an appealing option.

Then we have well water, which is sourced from underground aquifers. This water is extracted through a well and can vary significantly in quality depending on the location and surrounding environment. Well water often contains a diverse range of minerals and may also have contaminants, especially if the well is not properly maintained. Many people who rely on well water often have it tested regularly to ensure it's safe for consumption. While well water can be rich in minerals, it's essential to understand that it may also carry risks, particularly if it's not treated or filtered adequately.

Lastly, there's spring water. This type of water comes from natural springs, where water flows to the surface from underground sources. Spring water is typically bottled at the source and is known for its refreshing taste and natural mineral content. Unlike mineral water, which may have added minerals, spring water is often celebrated for its purity and the minerals it naturally contains. It's also worth noting that spring water must meet specific regulations to be labeled as such, ensuring that it's safe for consumption.

In summary, the differences between distilled, purified, mineral, well, and spring water lie in their sources, treatment processes, and mineral content. Distilled water is nearly pure, while purified water is treated for safety. Mineral water boasts natural minerals, well water comes from underground sources, and spring water flows naturally from springs. Each type has its unique characteristics and potential benefits, allowing consumers to choose based on their preferences and needs. Understanding these distinctions empowers us to make informed choices about the water we drink, ensuring we stay hydrated and healthy.

What Are Lawn Darts?

Lawn darts, often referred to as lawn dart games, are a classic outdoor activity that has entertained families and friends for decades. They consist of large, weighted darts designed to be thrown at a target on the ground, usually a circular ring or a designated area marked on the lawn. The game is simple in concept yet can be surprisingly competitive, making it a beloved pastime for gatherings, picnics, and backyard barbecues.

Historically, lawn darts have their roots in ancient games and sports, with similar throwing games dating back to ancient civilizations. However, the modern version of lawn darts became popular in the 1970s and 1980s, particularly in North America. The darts themselves are typically made of metal or plastic, featuring a pointed tip that is designed to stick into the ground when thrown correctly. The design allows for a satisfying thud as the dart lands, which adds to the excitement of the game.

The objective of lawn darts is straightforward: players take turns throwing their darts toward the target, aiming to score points based on where the darts land. Scoring systems can vary, but a common method awards points for darts that land inside the target area or close to it. Players often play to a predetermined score, and the first player or team to reach that score wins the game. This simplicity makes lawn darts accessible to players of all ages, from children to adults, and encourages friendly competition.

While lawn darts are a fun and engaging game, it's important to note that safety considerations have led to changes in their design and regulation over the years. In the 1980s, traditional lawn darts with sharp metal tips were associated with injuries, particularly among children. As a result, many countries, including the United States, imposed bans or restrictions on the sale of these hazardous versions. In their place, manufacturers began producing safer alternatives, often featuring rounded tips and softer materials designed to minimize the risk of injury.

Today, lawn darts are available in various styles and materials, catering to different preferences and safety standards. Some modern versions are made entirely of plastic, with no sharp edges, making them suitable for family-friendly play. Others incorporate colorful designs and themes, appealing to younger players and adding a festive touch to outdoor gatherings.

In addition to being a fun recreational activity, lawn darts can also promote physical coordination and hand-eye coordination skills. Players must develop their throwing techniques, adjusting their stance and grip to achieve the desired distance and accuracy. This aspect of the game can be particularly beneficial for children, as it encourages active play and helps develop motor skills in a social setting.

Moreover, lawn darts can serve as a means of bonding and socialization. The game fosters camaraderie among players, as they cheer each other on, celebrate victories, and share in the friendly banter that often accompanies competitive play. It can also be a platform for creating lasting memories, as families and friends gather for outdoor events, laughter echoing through the air as darts soar through the sky.

In conclusion, lawn darts are more than just a game; they are a cherished part of outdoor leisure culture that has stood the test of time. With their simple rules, engaging gameplay, and emphasis on social interaction, lawn darts continue to bring joy to people of all ages. As the game has evolved, so too have the materials and safety standards, ensuring that everyone can enjoy the thrill of throwing darts without the worry of injury. Whether played casually in a backyard or competitively in a tournament, lawn darts embody the spirit of outdoor fun and connection, reminding us of the importance of play in our lives.

What Is Jaywalking?

Jaywalking, a term that often evokes images of reckless pedestrians darting across busy streets, is more than just a colloquial expression; it embodies a complex interplay between urban life, traffic laws, and social behavior. At its core, jaywalking refers to the act of crossing a street unlawfully or without regard for the traffic signals and regulations in place. This behavior typically occurs when a pedestrian crosses a roadway at a location not designated for pedestrian traffic, such as crosswalks, or when they disregard traffic signals that dictate when it is safe to cross. The origins of the term date back to the early 20th century, with "jay" being a slang term for a simpleton or inexperienced person. In this context, a "jaywalker" was seen as someone who lacked the knowledge or awareness of proper street-crossing etiquette.

The legality of jaywalking varies significantly from one jurisdiction to another. In some places, it is strictly enforced, with police issuing citations to those who commit this infraction. In others, it may be treated more leniently, with law enforcement focusing on more pressing issues of public safety. The rationale behind jaywalking laws is rooted in the desire to protect both pedestrians and drivers. When pedestrians cross at inappropriate locations or disregard signals, they increase the risk of accidents. The statistics are telling; pedestrian fatalities have been on the rise in many urban areas, prompting cities to reassess their traffic laws and pedestrian safety measures.

Moreover, jaywalking is often seen as a reflection of the urban landscape itself. In densely populated cities, the design of streets and the availability of crosswalks can significantly influence pedestrian behavior. A lack of crosswalks or poorly timed traffic signals can lead to frustration among pedestrians, prompting them to take matters into their own hands and cross wherever they see fit. This is particularly common in cities where the distance between crosswalks is considerable or where traffic lights are slow to change. In such environments, the temptation to jaywalk can be strong, especially when pedestrians perceive the road to be clear.

Cultural attitudes toward jaywalking also play a significant role in its prevalence. In some cultures, jaywalking is viewed as a minor infraction, a common part of urban life that reflects the hustle and bustle of city living. In others, it may be seen as a serious violation of public safety, with social stigma attached to those who engage in it. This divergence can lead to interesting dynamics in pedestrian behavior, as individuals navigate the expectations of their environment. For instance, in cities with a strong emphasis on pedestrian rights and safety, jaywalking may be less common, as the infrastructure supports safe and efficient movement across streets.

Interestingly, the rise of technology has also impacted how we view and engage in jaywalking. With the advent of smartphones and navigation apps, pedestrians are more informed about their surroundings than ever before. However, this can lead to distraction, as individuals become engrossed in their devices while crossing streets. The phenomenon of "distracted walking" has become a growing concern, as pedestrians may fail to notice oncoming traffic or disregarded signals while focused on their screens.

Finally, addressing the issue of jaywalking requires a multifaceted approach that encompasses urban planning, public education, and law enforcement. Cities must prioritize pedestrian safety by designing roadways that account for foot traffic, ensuring that crosswalks are readily available and well-marked. Public awareness campaigns can help educate pedestrians about the importance of adhering to traffic laws and the potential consequences of jaywalking. Ultimately, the goal is to create a harmonious coexistence between pedestrians and vehicles, fostering an environment where safety is paramount and the streets are navigable for all. Jaywalking, while often seen as a simple act of defiance against traffic laws, serves as a reminder of the ongoing challenges and considerations in urban mobility.

Also by Michael Pollick

Michael Pollick's Proving Ground
Michael Pollick's Proving Ground
The Keepinnit Reels
The Keepinnit Reels 2: Acoustic Boogaloo
The Zero Sugar Keepinnit Reels
Professor Mike's Low-Flow Fountain Of Information
A Wise Geek's Guide To Everything

9 798227 509864